AF378222

Baron Marks of Woolwich

Cover and frontispiece: The first Baron Marks of
Woolwich – a portrait by R. W. Wolstenholme.

Baron Marks of Woolwich

International Entrepreneur, Engineer, Patent Agent and Politician (1858–1938)

MICHAEL R. LANE

QUILLER PRESS
London

First published by
Quiller Press Ltd
50 Albemarle Street,
London W1X 4BD

First published 1986

ISBN 0 907621 77 5

Set in 11 on 13 pt Baskerville by Galleon Photosetting, Ipswich, Suffolk.
Printed and bound in Great Britain by Camelot Press plc.

Contents

Author's Preface

The story of the First Baron Marks of Woolwich should have been written long ago, for it is a success story, one full of initiative, resolution, and of dedicated service to his fellow-men. It is strange that the events of his full and useful life were not recorded fifty years ago at the time of his death, when his achievements were fresh in the minds of his contemporaries and many of his personal papers were available for examination. Even the great international organization he founded in Lincoln's Inn Fields possesses remarkably few detailed records of his life.

This biography attempts to fill the void in our knowledge of this remarkable man. Published to coincide approximately with the 50th Anniversary of his death and the Centenary Celebrations of his firm, Marks & Clerk, it paints a picture of the career of a man of humble Puritan background, culminating in his elevation to the House of Lords. During his long and busy life he excelled as a professional engineer, a Chartered Patent Agent, a Member of the House of Commons, a successful businessman in both industry and commerce, and as a dedicated Christian devoted to the Congregational Church, the Sunday School Union and the Girls' Life Brigade. Throughout his life he applied the Christian belief in all his affairs, and although the benevolent head of a united family, the one great blessing to elude him was the joy of having children of his own.

Our tale begins in the Wellington district of Somerset when, in 1853, Lord Marks's father, a farm worker, left home in search of a better life. Members of the family are still to be found in the area and that is where research into this book started. During the next two years visits were made throughout the length and breadth of the country in search of information.

I should especially like to thank the following for their patient assistance and hospitality. Firstly, Mrs Gladys Russell, Aunt Ella to the family, now living in retirement at Flete in Devonshire. She is Lord Marks's brother Edward's only surviving child, and provided a great deal of valuable information, including her father's Journal, covering the vital period when Lord Marks left Tangye Brothers employ and put up his plate as a Consulting Engineer in Birmingham. Her nephew, Godfrey Marks, a grandson of Lord Marks's brother Edward and now living in Newcastle upon Tyne, was of invaluable assistance, reading and most professionally criticizing my manuscript. Aunt Ella's niece and Godfrey's cousin, Miss Sheila Marks, living at Ilkley, was also most kind and provided many of the photographs used to illustrate this book. Lord Marks's Ward, 'Queenie' Usher's son, Michael, living in Lichfield, provided a host of anecdotal stories, vivid recollections and photographs of family holidays spent at Lord and Lady Marks's seaside homes.

During my researches each of Lord Marks's cliff railways and the site of the now defunct Matlock steep incline tramway were visited, with the exception of Budapest. Time and expense precluded the latter, although during a recent visit to Belgrade it was confirmed that the railway still operates very much as it was originally built. Recollections of my two visits to Lynton & Lynmouth will long remain, not only because of the sheer beauty of the district, but the present Director and General Manager, Mr Bob Jones, a grandson of the original building contractor, was a most pleasant and unforgettable character. It is unfortunate that the printed history of the railway available in booklet form makes no reference to Lord Marks, giving all the credit to Sir George Newnes and Bob Jones. Hopefully, this will be corrected during the railway's not-too-far-distant Centenary Celebrations.

Other visits were made to Padstow and Lord Marks's former North Cornwall constituency, to Birmingham where the Marks's success story started, and to Eltham, where the brothers George and Edward Marks were born. All these visits included many hours in local reference libraries and similar sources of information. Marks & Clerk also provided all the help and willing assistance possible. But, I must especially and most sincerely thank Mr Norman Waddleton, the recently retired Senior Partner of Marks & Clerk, my mentor and inspiration for the project.

Finally, I should like to express my appreciation to Mrs Julia Warren, who expertly translated my hand-written manuscript onto a word processor. Also, to Mr Hugh Tempest-Radford, who 'lightly' edited and improved my manuscript, and to my publisher, Mr Jeremy Greenwood. It has been a joy working with all three. If there are any errors or I have unwittingly misrepresented any person in the course of recounting the Marks's story, the responsibility is entirely mine.

Michael R. Lane

Street House, Boxted, Bury St Edmunds   August 1986

Foreword

by Norman Waddleton

Lord Marks had no heirs and I never met him but as his spiritual heir for twenty years it is a great pleasure for me to write this foreword to Michael Lane's biography, not only because this account of his life is an interesting and informative study of an eminent Victorian but because the book helps us to view the life and career of Lord Marks in a proper perspective. Up until now his reputation has perhaps been somewhat eclipsed by the greater reputation of his lifelong partner Sir Dugald Clerk, who achieved lasting recognition for his invention of the two-stroke engine.

Michael Lane is exceptionally well qualified to tell this story. He is an established author of books on industrial archaeology and is well known for his work to preserve the records of our industrial archaeological inheritance. There is an added bonus in that he even has, through his own family, personal contacts with members of Lord Marks's family and links with the Somerset area from which Lord Marks's forebears came.

As well as telling the story of Lord Marks and of his achievements this book is intended by the timing of its publication to be a centenary celebration of the time when Lord Marks first set himself up as a self-employed consulting engineer – a man of his time who is well worth remembering, and not merely by those who still benefit from his wisdom and foresight.

Chapter 1

George Croydon Marks (1858–1938)

The unexpected death of Charles II in February 1685 and the ensuing fateful decisions of his illegitimate son, James Scott, Duke of Monmouth, left their mark upon the people of Taunton and surrounding districts for many generations. Monmouth had been well beloved by his father and was living a life of pleasure in the Hague, accompanied by the beautiful Lady Wentworth, as the guest of William of Orange. He suddenly found that henceforward he must deal not with a father who would forgive anything, but with his Papist Uncle James, who forgave nothing.

As soon as the news was received in Holland, King William insisted that Monmouth return immediately to England, where he became surrounded by those desperate to preserve the Protestant Monarchy. 'Claim your rights,' they urged, 'Now or never!' In May, Monmouth and a small group of Whig supporters gambled for the throne. Setting sail for the West Country in three small ships, they landed at Lyme Regis on 11 June. They were at once welcomed by the local people and Monmouth issued a proclamation asserting the validity of his mother, Lucy Waters's marriage to Charles, denouncing James as a usurper. Within days some 6000 ardent supporters enlisted in his rebel army and made a long march through Taunton and Bridgwater towards Bristol. The then second city promptly closed its gates against them. A month after the landing, regular troops, loyal to the new King, converged upon the Bridgwater area, led by a former French emigrant, whom James had created Earl of Feversham.

There seems little doubt that despite the enthusiasm of the common people, Monmouth knew that his adventure was doomed. In a last desperate act, he launched a surprise night attack on Feversham's forces camped at Sedgemoor. But, even before the fierce battle was resolved, Monmouth fled the field, leaving the Somerset peasants to die for him. He was eventually captured and summarily executed. Judge Jeffreys's notorious Bloody Assize held in Taunton, then took vengeance on the rank and file of the rebels.

The tales of executions and mass deportations to Barbados momentarily sickened the nation, but the majority soon rallied around the Establishment, giving their support to the new King. They blamed the West Country non-conformists for the ill-advised and badly led rebellion.

Throughout the reign of Charles II non-conformists continued to suffer intermittent persecution, the victims coming mainly from the lower and middle classes residing in the Shires, especially those in the West Country. This prejudice was more for political and social reasons, than from genuinely religious motives, and persisted well into the nineteenth century. It continued even after the repeal of the notorious Test Act in 1828 which, for the first time since 1673, allowed Dissenters the privilege of a University education and the right to participate in most other aspects of public life. In its later stages, the persecution was frequently due simply to jealousy, for the non-conformists, especially the Quakers, demonstrated remarkable commercial acumen and thrift enabling them to survive the periods of economic depression which plagued the first half of the nineteenth century.

Typical non-conformists of their time, struggling to establish their personal and economic bourgeois independence, were the Marks family of West Buckland, a hamlet near Wellington in Somerset, now straddled by the M5 motorway. Robert Marks, born in 1774, and his wife Margaret were farmers and ardent members of the Congregational sect. Their son, Michael, born in 1797, and his wife Harriott, who came from nearby Milverton, followed in their footsteps as hardworking decent people, deriving their livelihood from the land, whilst persistent in their religious faith. On 23 January 1834, three years before Queen Victoria ascended the throne, Harriott presented Michael with a son whom they christened William. We know virtually nothing of the boy's childhood except that at an early age, he was sent to work on a farm in the Blackdown Hills, a few miles south of West Buckland. Whether this was intended to give William a broader experience of farming than his father could provide, or whether it was due to economic necessity, we cannot speculate. In later years, William described the pressures and unpleasantness he encountered from time to time at the hands of the local Establishment because of his Non-conformist faith. At the age of nineteen, he left the district and travelled to Bristol in search of work.

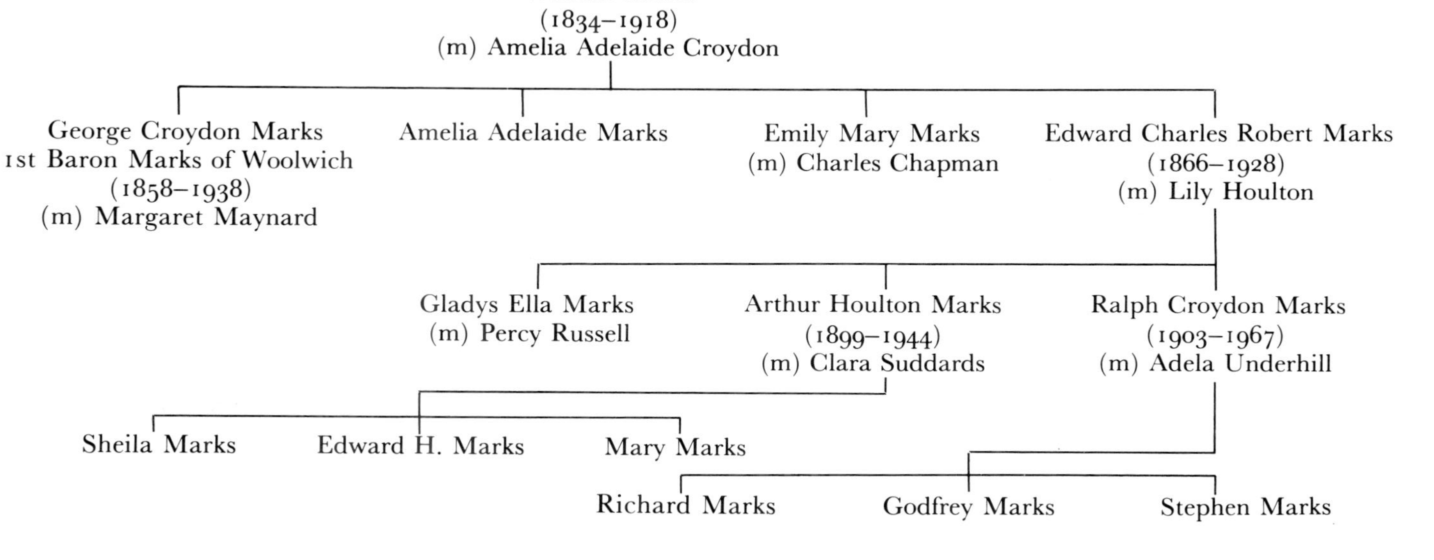

The Marks family tree.

In 1854, William met and fell in love with Amelia Adelaide Croydon, and three years later she became his wife. Amelia lived with relatives at Staple Hill, Mangotsfield, a suburb of Bristol, both her parents having died some years earlier. Her father, Thomas Croydon (1788–1842), was born at Crediton in Devonshire, and her mother, formerly Mary Jones (1790–1839), came from Lynton on the North Devon coast. Her cousin, Bob Jones, played an important rôle in the Marks story thirty years later, working closely with William Marks's two sons as the Contractor to the Lynton & Lynmouth Cliff Railway Company. It is said that the Croydon family were at first apprehensive about Amelia's friendship with the country lad she had met at the local Congregational church. They had cherished the hope that their ward would make a 'good marriage', and were justifiably concerned about William's career prospects.

It appears that the young couple agreed to a period of separation, for in 1855, William Marks obtained employment at the Royal Arsenal, Woolwich, in East London, where he remained for the next forty-three years. He quickly established himself as a trustworthy and hard-working employee and within two years felt sufficiently secure to marry his beloved Amelia. The wedding took place in Bristol on 22 September 1857, with the Croydon family's blessing. Initially, they set up home in a tiny cottage adjoining Eltham churchyard, in what is now Well Hall Road. Later, when the children arrived, they removed to 2 Myrtle Cottages, Back Lane, Eltham, a bungalow described as a dairy cottage. In subsequent years, three generations of the Marks family recalled with pleasure their memories of life at Myrtle Cottage, for undoubtedly it was always a happy, united, Christian home. William and Amelia Marks proved to be excellent home builders, pillars of the local Congregational church which they attended for over sixty years and thoroughly good neighbours, yet they always remained humble and unpretentious. Amelia maintained close contacts with her family in the West Country, and whenever possible visited her cousins at Lynton. William, however, appears to have severed all connection with Somerset, although to this day some of his kinsmen farm in the Wellington area.

It was into this environment that their first child was born on 9 June 1858. Christened George Croydon Marks, the boy was the first of eight children, four of whom sadly died in infancy. Two

William Marks (1834–1918), Lord Marks's father.

sisters, Emily Mary and Amelia Adelaide, and the youngest boy, Edward Charles Robert, survived. George Marks developed as a very normal boy in an economically poor, but spiritually rich home, and few could have foreseen the diverse and distinguished career ahead.

A new day school opened in Elm Terrace, Eltham, in 1864, and George Marks and his life-long friends Alfred and Alexander Smith were amongst the first pupils. Often, in later life, George spoke kindly of Mr Penrose, the Principal, and his assistant, Mr Baker, acknowledging the very considerable debt he owed the school. Apparently, from an early age, he declared his wish to become an engineer, and books and magazines dealing with mechanical subjects became his main leisure interest. At the age of thirteen, by arrangement with his father's employers, he entered the Royal Arsenal School in Woolwich, which enabled him to continue his basic education, whilst at the same time gaining valuable practical experience in the modern, well-equipped workshops and drawing-office at the Arsenal.

In common with other apprentices under sixteen years of age, he attended the Royal Arsenal School one day each week and evening classes four evenings a week, taking both science and arts subjects. During his first year he won the School's 3rd Prize, and in his second year he gained the coveted 1st Prize. Work in the Royal Laboratory, where George was initially employed, started at 6.00 a.m., and he was paid one penny an hour for 56 hours' work each week. Following a probationary period, the rate was increased to seven shillings (35p) a week. George was never physically robust, and these long working hours, combined with his attendance at evening classes, imposed a severe strain upon him, and more than once he became ill.

Many years later when distributing the prizes at Woolwich Polytechnic shortly after becoming Lord Marks of Woolwich, he recounted how, during a period of illness, his fellow apprentices had a whip-round and presented him with £4, which was equivalent to his lost earnings, enabling him to purchase urgently needed books. George Marks never forgot this kindness, and after presenting the prizes he donated a cheque for £1000 to be invested for the benefit of the Woolwich engineering apprentices.

Colonel Milward, then Superintendent of the Royal Laboratory, spotted George's ability and conscientious approach to life and instructed that he should be given the opportunity of learning whatever trade he wished. Having chosen mechanical engineering, George was placed under the supervision of one of the Arsenal's best mechanics. He spent time on the bench learning to use hand tools, developing an eye for flatness and symmetry. Later, he was taught the art of turning and screw-cutting on the centre lathe, and the operation of the shaper, the planing machine and the recently introduced milling machine. This was followed by training in the Boiler Shop and the department producing special tooling.

In 1875, the prominent northern industrialist Sir Joseph Whitworth financed a scheme for an experimental period of four years, whereby three Exhibitions were to be competed for annually at King's College, University of London. The Exhibitions were open to young men who were 'possessed of a certain measure of mechanical aptitude and of a dexterity in the use of tools and are desirous of training in the principles of pure and applied science.' The scheme was widely advertised in the trade journals and became one of the most sought-after opportunities for Engineering students.

William and Amelia Marks outside Myrtle Cottage.

George Marks was amongst the first batch of candidates selected for interview. In due course, after sitting the Entrance Examination, he was the first to be offered a place and entered Kings College in September 1875. The Royal Arsenal retained George on its books, which enabled him to resume work during the vacations. During these periods, he lived at home and was given work in the Arsenal's machinery breakdown and repair department. Considerable overtime was available to augment the normal rates of pay and George was able to double his meagre income.

Upon the successful completion of two years' study at King's College, George Marks returned to full-time employment at the Royal Asenal, working in the Millwrights Department. One suspects that it was not long before he became impatient with manual work. Having obtained an academic qualification, he naturally sought to broaden his horizons and to gain experience in new fields. In 1878, against his father's advice, George left the Arsenal and took a position in the Drawing Office at Easton & Andersons, General Engineers, in nearby Erith. He was employed as a junior draughtsman, engaged in the preparation of component drawings for a variety of projects.

Whilst George was working at Erith, the Company was involved in a series of experiments initiated by the Institution of Mechanical Engineers, laying the foundations for a rational theory of lubrication. The project was led by Mr Beauchamp Tower of the Metropolitan Railway, and Easton & Andersons manufactured the special machinery used in the tests. Tower was able to demonstrate that a journal rotating in a bearing acted as a pump, dragging the oil round to the point of greatest pressure, creating a film of lubricant which served to carry the load. He established the principle that oil should be supplied to a bearing at the point of minimum pressure, and that the motion of the shaft itself could be relied upon to carry it round to where it was most wanted.

Two years later George Marks moved on and accepted the post as Chief Draughtsman with Ross & Walpole in Dublin. In later life he rarely referred to his two years' residence in Dublin, probably because 1880 was not a good year for a young Non-conformist Englishman with Liberal leanings to seek employment in Ireland. During that year, no less than 10,450 tenant farmers were evicted from their homes, and 2590 outrages, including the brutal murder of Lord Mountmorres, were recorded. The Irish Nationalist leader Parnell urged that anyone taking a farm from which the tenant had been evicted should be ostracized and treated as a leper as of old. The first person to be so treated was a certain Captain Boycott, a land agent from County Mayo, and a new word was added to the English language.

The Irish problem was as intractable then as now, and Parliament seemed quite unable to deal with the situation. An Irish cynic once said, 'The English are fools trying to solve the Irish problem, for every time they propose a solution, we have altered the problem!' Perhaps this is the reason that, in spite of his first-hand experience, George Marks never allowed himself to be drawn into the 'Irish Question' during his long Parliamentary career.

Shortly after he completed his studies at King's College, George and his old school friend Alfred Smith became teachers at Eltham Congregational Church Sunday School. They were assisted by two charming young ladies living in the district and a close relationship developed between the four, such that most onlookers regarded their eventual marriage as a foregone conclusion. Whilst with Easton & Andersons, George Marks proposed to and was accepted by one of the girls. Margaret Maynard was the eldest child of Thomas Maynard, a Bath boatbuilder, and his wife Adelaide. They had a family of two daughters and three sons. The marriage took place on 30 July 1881, to the great delight of both families. The ceremony, for reasons which are not now clear, took place at Watford Congregational Church, and set the seal on a union which was to last fifty-seven years.

Margaret was always known to family and friends as Maggie, and throughout their long life together, she was always at George's side, quite often unobtrusively, but nevertheless wholeheartedly supporting him. It is not known whether Maggie returned to Dublin with George or, indeed, when he actually terminated his employment with Ross & Walpole. However, it does seem clear that at the time of his marriage he resolved to seek new employment in order to set up a home in England for his bride. His endeavours were soon rewarded, and in the early part of 1882 he was offered a promising post with Tangye Ltd of Cornwall Works in the Smethwick district of Birmingham. George and Maggie acquired a house in Hall Road, Lozells, then a pleasant residential suburb on the north side of the city. By this date Tangye Ltd had established an enviable record internationally as mechanical engineers, and was the type of company with whom any ambitious young engineer would have been proud to be associated.

The firm had been founded in January 1858 by the brothers James, Joseph, Richard and George Tangye, who were later joined by their youngest brother, Edward. They were all born in Illogan, the same Cornish village as Richard Trevithick, the inventor of the high-pressure steam engine. The Tangye family, like their neighbours, the distinguished engineers Harveys of Hayle, were Quakers. Leaving school at the age of twelve, James Tangye resolved to follow in his maternal grandfather's footsteps and become an engineer. He secured employment at the Cornish Copper Company's Copperhouse Foundry in Hayle, where he was employed upon the manufacture of bridge components for I. K. Brunel. These were used firstly for spanning the Thames at Hungerford, and later on the Clifton suspension bridge over the River Avon at Bristol. During this period he was fortunate to work under the supervision of the great man, gaining much valuable experience and receiving from him suggestions for future work testing the strength of iron plates by hydraulic press. Shortly after the brothers had established their own works in Birmingham, it was to James Tangye that Brunel turned when all traditional methods for launching his great ship *Great Eastern* failed. Large jacks were delivered to the site at Millwall on the Thames in record time and the ship was successfully launched. In later life, Richard Tangye, in his autobiography, described the arrival of Brunel's assistant at their little workshop late one dark evening with an order for the jacks. For the brothers it was literally fortune knocking on their door, for they were then practically unknown in the trade, but Brunel had remembered young James from his days at the Copperhouse Foundry. The subsequent performance of the Tangye hydraulic jacks was such that it provided the foundation of the great business which blossomed under their control in the second half of the nineteenth century. It was James's proud boast, 'We launched *Great Eastern*, and she launched us.'

The four eldest brothers had come to Birmingham originally in 1855, when James was appointed Works Manager at the Quaker Thomas Worsdell's Railway Works in Berkley Street. This firm manufactured cranes, overhead traversers, winches, jacks, material testing machines, early steam road rollers and locomotives for the Potteries, Shrewsbury & North Wales Railway. The Worsdells were a remarkable family too, for Thomas's father built the tender for Stephenson's 'Rocket', and his two brothers, Nathaniel and George, were both distinguished railway engineers. Two of Nathaniel's sons, Thomas William and Wilson Worsdell, were successively Locomotive Superintendents on the North Eastern Railway and pioneers in the use of the compound principle in railway locomotives.

Initially, the Tangye brothers concentrated on manufacturing hydraulic jacks and various types of lifting tackle, including the Weston Block. Then followed the successful Tangye steam pump, based on an American design brought over from the United States by Edward Tangye. It was the development of hydraulically operated machinery, however, which gave the Company its greatest impetus. Later, George Tangye designed a range of steam engines in which all the components were as simple as possible. The resulting high degree of standardization enabled the components to be produced economically in large numbers. So successful were all these activities that extensive additions to the Cornwall Works were soon required.

In 1872 a serious split occurred in the family resulting in James and Edward Tangye taking early retirement and returning to their native Cornwall. The other brothers continued to run the business, and became well-known public figures in Birmingham. George Tangye acquired Heathfield Hall, James Watts's old home in Handsworth, where he lived for over forty years. He was custodian of Watts's historic papers for some time, until a permanent home could be found for them in the City.

It was into this environment, with its close connections with the beginning of the Industrial Revolution, that George Croydon Marks took his first steps in management at the age of twenty-four. Within a short time he was appointed Manager of the Lifting Machinery Department, reporting directly to Mr George Tangye. The work involved long hours and extensive travelling visiting customers, but Marks quickly gained his employer's complete confidence. In 1883 he was associated with the design and construction of a Cliff Railway at Saltburn-by-the-Sea, operating on the water balance principle. Four years later, while still employed at the Cornwall Works, he was consulted about a similar scheme at Lynton and Lynmouth, on the North Devon coast, but this story belongs to Chapter 4. By this time George had become recognized as an expert in the design and manufacture of all types of lifts and hoists. He was named in several patents filed by the Tangye brothers in the years 1882–87, and by the middle of the decade, his future as an engineer seemed assured. Both George and his wife settled happily in Birmingham. They made many new friends, but it was George's job, and their active membership of the Soho Hill Congregational Church and Sunday School, which provided the centre-piece of their lives. Suddenly, however, something appeared to go wrong with relationships at the Cornwall Works, and on 27 June 1887, George Marks resigned.

Chapter 2

Edward Marks (1866–1928) and Dugald Clerk (1854–1932)

We must now turn our attention to two people who played a leading rôle in George Marks's successful career. The oft-repeated cliché, 'Behind every successful man is a woman', may be true, but equally behind every successful person with responsibilities there is a team of loyal colleagues and supporters. They may be family or friends, business partners, assistants, or even domestic staff. This inner circle is critical to success and throughout his life George Marks was wise and extremely fortunate in his choice of associates.

Edward Charles Robert Marks, George's younger brother, and Dugald Clerk, later Sir Dugald Clerk, KBE, the distinguished academic, were his closest collaborators for over forty years. Both were actively associated with his business affairs from 1887 until their deaths. George always naturally assumed the rôle of Senior Partner, and no formal agreement existed between the three men until 1894. The devoted service and wise counsel both gave throughout their association was undoubtedly a major factor in George Marks's subsequent success. Together with his wife, Maggie, Edward and Dugald Clerk were his closest confidants in all matters.

Edward Marks was eight years younger than George. He was born at Eltham on 8 December 1866, and his early upbringing closely matched that of his elder brother. He was adored by his two sisters and, one suspects, often spoilt by them, although they never relinquished the special authority given to elder sisters. The earliest surviving reference to Edward is in a letter to George, written by his mother while visiting Aunt Jones at her home, The Lyndale Hotel in Lynmouth. She wrote, 'I took dear baby on the beach the other morning and dipped him right into some sea water, but he did not like it very much!' In 1880, he followed in George's footsteps and entered the Royal Arsenal, Woolwich. He was apprenticed for five years, spending time in the different departments, while continuing his education in classes arranged by the old Science and Art Department in the Arsenal school.

In 1885, Edward secured employment at Tangye's Cornwall

Works as a Junior Draughtsman working in the section responsible for crane and lift design. Initially, much of his time was devoted to developing a new grab and hoist proposed by his brother. In the Victorian era, nepotism was not confined to the proprietors of business enterprises, and it was not infrequent for trusted employees to be encouraged to recruit other members of their family. The system had merit, for often family ties and loyalties added greatly to the efficiency of the organization, especially when the new applicant had received his early training and experience elsewhere. Edward rented lodgings in the Soho Hill area of Birmingham and, like his brother, became closely involved with the activities of the local Congregational Church and Sunday School.

Edward Marks was always meticulous in his ways and during the two and a half years spent at the Cornwall Works he maintained a journal, recording his thoughts and daily activities. Fortuitously, this not only describes events at a turning-point in the three men's lives, but paints a fascinating picture of a young professional engineer's life 100 years ago. Birmingham was then widely known as 'The City of a thousand trades' and 'The Workshop of the World'. England had enjoyed peace for thirty years, indeed it had not been faced with a serious threat from its neighbours for nearly seventy years. Technical developments were taking place at an unprecedented rate and generally the future looked promising for the majority of the British people. Birmingham in particular was growing rapidly, and although the rate of growth precipitated some serious social problems, the administration and control of the City was in the hands of capable, far-seeing and caring men.

The diversity of Birmingham's industries in the 1880s enabled George and Edward Marks to obtain a wide knowledge of the contemporary industrial scene, for most Midlands factories were then using some piece of plant or machinery manufactured at the Cornwall Works. Individually motorized, electrically driven machinery belongs to the twentieth century, and Tangye steam engines and gas engines were used extensively for driving the miles of overhead line shafting which then provided power through pulleys and leather belts to the individual pieces of machinery. Most factories required lifts and hoists for moving work between floors in multi-storey brick buildings. Heavy industries, the railways and canals all used cranes. Hydraulically operated machinery was coming increasingly into use in a variety of processes and operations, and the hydraulic jack became standard equipment for the millwrights employed in every factory. The metal industries commonly used Tangye materials testing equipment in their development and quality control departments.

First among the local trades in 1880 were the various branches of the brassfoundry industry, in which about 11,000 people were employed. The principal articles produced were plumbers' brassfoundry, general household fittings, lamps and chandeliers, bells, bedsteads, ordnance, naval, railway and ecclesiastical brasswork. The largest and one of the oldest-established firms was R. W. Winfield & Company, whose works occupied the present site of the City's Hall of Memory in Broad Street. The author clearly remembers seeing one of Winfield's old gas engines at work in the early 1930s, providing power for the line shafting driving twenty brass-finishers' lathes.

The gun trade ranked second among Birmingham's industries at this time, employing over 10,000 people. Although the industry had declined following the establishment of the Government-owned Enfield Small Arms Factory in Middlesex, the 1880 Annual Report of the Guardians of the Proof House confirmed that 558,000 locally made gun barrels had been proved during the year. The largest firm in the district was the Birmingham Small Arms Company, founded in 1861 on a 25-acre site in Small Heath. The company later became world renowned as manufacturers of bicycles, motor cycles and machine tools.

Button manufacture was flourishing in Birmingham when James Watt and his wealthy partner, Matthew Boulton, established the Soho Foundry in 1764. It was still a major industry when George Marks came to the city 120 years later. Electro-plating was another industry, which in its day brought fame to the area. In 1838, a young German engineer, William Siemens, later Sir William, a Past President of the Institution of Mechanical Engineers, sold to the old-established firm Elkington & Company, a process developed by his brother Werner for the electro-deposition of metals. Elkington's factory was located in Newhall Street, and today houses Birmingham's splendid Museum of Science and Industry. Soon the very high-quality silver-plated work manufactured by the firm received worldwide acclaim.

Other prosperous Birmingham trades included the manufacture of woodscrews. Messrs Nettlefold, who were largely owned by the

Chamberlain family, produced 200,000 gross a week in 1882. Cut nail making, die-sinking, wire drawing, cable manufacture and jewellery of all types, also featured prominently. Messrs Horsfall of Hay Mills produced the first Atlantic cable, and at the time were the largest wire and cable manufacturers in the world. Another important local industry was the manufacture of glass, dominated by Chance Brothers. Specialist glassmakers F. & C. Osler achieved worldwide fame for their ornamental and stained glass. They are especially remembered for the magnificent Crystal Fountain, regarded by many as the centrepiece of the Great Exhibition held in the Crystal Palace, Hyde Park, in 1851.

Finally, mention must be made of the steel pen-nib industry, for it is said that in the 1880s two firms, Messrs Gillott and Perry & Company, were responsible for the production of 20 million nibs every week. It is worth noting that the people of Birmingham were familiar with mass-production techniques twenty or thirty years before the United States of America began to organize its manu-facturing industries for volume production. The owner of Perry & Company, Sir Josiah Mason, used his wealth for the benefit of Birmingham, and became one of its greatest Victorian benefactors. He gave them a fine College of Science, in Edmund Street, near the City's Doric columned Town Hall, and a vast Gothic-style orphanage at Erdington.

In later years all these industries, and most of the companies mentioned, employed Marks and Clerk as Patent Agents. George Marks and his colleagues were at the centre of industrial enterprise and innovation and were sufficiently alert and entrepreneurial to capitalize upon the many friendships and contacts made whilst in Tangye's employ, but we are moving somewhat ahead of our story.

Edward Marks's journal provides us with vivid glimpses of his private life and of his relationship with his family. Undoubtedly, he was devoted to his brother and sister-in-law. When he left home for the first time as a young man of nineteen years, it was Maggie Marks who found and approved his lodgings in Soho. The brothers' working day was long and fully occupied them for six days each week, the seventh day being devoted entirely to their religious affairs at Soho Hill Congregational Church where George had been appointed a Deacon. During this period George undertook a number of preaching engagements and was described as a capable and convincing local preacher. A typical Sunday started with adult classes at 7.30 a.m., followed by the morning Sunday School Classes and Morning Service. In the afternoon George, Maggie and Edward attended the main session of the Sunday School, George having become the Superintendent soon after his arrival in Birmingham. In the evening George held a 'Ragged School' for the poor children of the City.

In the summer months, Sundays usually ended with a walk through the residential district of Handsworth, which today is largely occupied by the City's immigrant population. In the winter, they returned to George and Maggie's home and read before the fire. Edward's tastes appear to have been classical, whereas George seems to have confined his reading to technical books and magazines. Throughout his life George Marks was a man without hobbies or leisure pursuits, and it was only in his declining years that he derived immense pleasure from his Japanese gardens at Carrick Grange, Sevenoaks, and Cerne Abbas, Bournemouth.

From his arrival in Birmingham, until he resigned from Tangye's employment in 1887, George Marks was a part-time member of the teaching staff at the Birmingham and Midland Institute in Paradise Street. In later life it was said that all over the Kingdom there were students who had profited greatly from his lectures in engineering and applied mathematics. The Institute had been founded in 1853 out of the old Philosophical Institution and its new premises were formally opened by the Prince Consort in November 1855. It provided the City with the privileges of an excellent Literary Society, and classes for the study of languages, literature and science at exceedingly low fees. Edward Marks was a student at the Institute's evening classes for three sessions, and in November 1888 was awarded the Queen's Prize for advanced metallurgy.

Often, after attending the Institute, the two brothers retired to the Cobden Temperance Hotel in Corporation Street for supper and a chat. Clearly, Edward was at all times completely in his elder brother's confidence. They were also in the habit of spending their holidays together. Twice a year, in midsummer and at Christmas, the Cornwall Works closed and the three usually visited William and Amelia Marks at Myrtle Cottage, Eltham. On such visits, George frequently accompanied his father, who was now a Foreman, on a nostalgic visit to the Royal Arsenal. Periodically, Maggie went away on her own to stay with her sister, Mrs Pearce, and her children, who lived in Berkhamsted.

Edward Marks (1866–1928), Lord Marks's brother.

During Bank Holiday breaks from work, Edward frequently went on an expedition to explore some Midland beauty spot. He recorded in his journal visits to Stratford-upon-Avon, and to the Clent Hills, and on another occasion he visited Chipping Norton. One August Bank Holiday Monday he and a friend walked 35 miles. They climbed the 750-ft-high Barr Beacon, with its magnificent views of the surrounding countryside, and crossed Sutton Park, a popular beauty spot given to the people of the Royal Borough of Sutton Coldfield by a grateful King Henry VIII. They reached the cathedral city of Lichfield in time for lunch and returned home to Soho exhausted in the late evening.

Edward was extremely observant of everything around him, especially of things mechanical. He recorded a journey on one of Birmingham's new steam trams, and he compared at length the relative merits of the London & North Western Railway and the Midland Railway. Both ran trains out of Birmingham's New Street Station. Clearly, Edward favoured the Midland's splendid clerestory roofed, plush upholstered carriages and complimented the Company upon its excellent time-keeping. In May 1887 he visited Edinburgh for the first time, and faithfully recorded details of the nine-hour train journey which took him over Shap Summit. The thrilling climax of this visit was the opportunity of inspecting

Sir John Fowler's masterpiece the new Forth Bridge whilst under construction. He vividly described the scene, including the extensive workshops and facilities provided for fabricating the vast steel tubes and other structures used in the construction of the bridge.

A National Holiday was declared to celebrate the Queen's Jubilee on 21 June 1887, and the Cornwall Works closed for a long week-end. On Jubilee Day, George and Edward went to the Malvern Hills to see the lighting of a huge beacon, one of a chain arranged across the Kingdom. The following day they travelled to Manchester, to visit a trade and industry exhibition held in Trafford Park. They went by the Midland Railway route through the Peak District, and were both greatly impressed by the beauty of this now defunct line.

Shortly before the Queen's Jubilee, Edward recorded in his journal his concern at events taking place at the Cornwall Works. It appears the Company was experiencing the effects of the recession in the manufacturing industries, which followed in the wake of the Great Agricultural Depression. Using the modern jargon of the business world, it appears that the Company's cash flow was in an unhealthy state. The Company Secretary, Mr Parkins, tried to bring the situation under control by advocating drastic reductions in manpower and overhead expenditure. These proposals, which no doubt were in some degree necessary, were implemented in an arbitrary and unsympathetic manner, resulting in the resignation of Mr Ewen, the Works Manager. This in turn caused discontent throughout the Company, arising from divided loyalties and feelings of insecurity. Mr George Tangye discussed the situation with George Marks, but when he insisted that George should become assistant to Ewen's successor, George, after careful consideration, felt compelled to resign.

The traumatic events at the Cornwall Works in the spring of 1887 undoubtedly brought George Marks and his colleague Dugald Clerk closer together. Both were heads of Departments in the Company, and both had similar vested interests in its future. Following an agonizing period of consultation with Clerk and prayerful thought and discussion with Maggie Marks, George decided to leave the Company. Without delay, he put up his plate as an independent Consulting Engineer at offices in Temple Street, in the centre of Birmingham. George saw in his former colleague someone who could add lustre to this new enterprise, and it is clear that an understanding already existed between the two men when George resigned from Tangyes.

Dugald Clerk was born in Glasgow on 31 March 1854, the eldest son of Donald Clerk and Martha Symington, the second daughter of John Brown of Glasgow. At the age of 14 Dugald entered his father's factory, gaining practical experience as a machinist before starting a two-year apprenticeship with a local engineering firm, H. D. Robinson & Co. Ltd. Concurrently, he attended evening classes at the West of Scotland Technical College, and in 1871, upon the completion of his apprenticeship, he commenced full-time studies at the Andersonian College in Glasgow, reading Chemistry and Physics. He proved to be a brilliant student, passing all his examinations with distinction. In 1874 he had no difficulty obtaining a post as lecturer at the Yorkshire College in Leeds, working under the direction of Professor Sir T. E. Thorpe. The following year an opportunity arose for him to return to Glasgow as assistant to Dr J. E. Ellis, the Young Professor of Technical Chemistry at the Royal Technical College.

Originally Dugald Clerk had intended to specialize in Chemical Engineering, but whilst working under Dr Ellis, on the making of paraffin oils, his attention was drawn to a small gas engine in a joiners' workshop in Glasgow, manufactured by the Belgian engineer Étienne Lenoir. In the years 1860–65, Lenoir produced several hundred of these engines in his small Paris factory, and undoubtedly, their subsequent development, which continued simultaneously in France, Germany and the United Kingdom, was one of the most important events in the history of mechanical engineering.

In the Lenoir engine the gas was admitted alternately to each end of the horizontal cylinder for a part of the piston stroke, then ignited by an electric spark at atmospheric pressure, and expanded during the remainder of the stroke. This produced two explosions, one on each side of the piston, for each revolution of the crank. After ignition and expansion of the gas, the return stroke was used for exhausting one side of the piston, while induction, ignition and expansion took place on the other. The cylinder was water-cooled, and conventional steam-engine-type slide valves were used for controlling the admission and exhaust.

It was soon recognized that the lack of compression and incomplete expansion of the gas, coupled with excessive heat loss

Sir Dugald Clerk, KBE, FRS (1854–1932), Lord Marks's original partner.

through the cylinder walls, caused the engines to be uneconomical. In 1862 a Frenchman, Beau de Rochas, proposed a four-stroke cycle of operations as a solution. However, it was not until 1876 that a German engineer Dr Nicholas Otto actually produced a gas engine which was to prove the practicability of de Rochas's ideas. The engine was an immediate success and laid the foundations for the modern petrol engine used today in the majority of motor-cars. By 1885, no less than 45,000 engines were built under licence in Germany, England, France and the United States, having a combined power output of more than 400,000 horse power.

In the same year, while still employed at the Royal Technical College, Dugald Clerk commenced work on an alternative system, and for the next fifteen years he devoted the greater part of his life to the study of thermodynamics and the development of the internal combustion engine. Soon he abandoned the academic world and joined Thomson, Sterne & Company at the Crown Ironworks in

Glasgow, who had been engaged upon the development of the internal combustion engine for the previous twelve years.

The system Dugald Clerk proposed provided for the exhausting of the single acting cylinder at the end of the expansion stroke, and the admission of the unburnt gas at the beginning of the compression stroke, necessitating a displacement pump or the equivalent, to deliver the new charge at low pressure into the main cylinder. Originally, he arranged for the exhaust gases to pass through ports in the cylinder wall, which were uncovered when the piston reached the end of its stroke. The operations of suction, compression, expansion and exhaust took place during two strokes of the piston and one revolution of the crank, becoming known generally as the Two-Stroke Cycle. In the alternative Otto system the same operation took place in four strokes of the piston and two revolutions of the crank, hence the term Four-Stroke Cycle. Neither the Four-Stroke Cycle nor the Two-Stroke Cycle has established superiority over the other, and today both types of engine are manufactured in vast quantities, the majority burning petrol instead of gas.

Dugald Clerk described his first gas engine in his patent No. 252 filed in 1877. The Two-Stroke Cycle, as we know it today, was the subject of his further well-known patent No. 1089 of 1881, which described the world's first compression explosion engine having a power impulse every revolution. The prototype engine was coupled to an early shunt-wound electrical dynamo manufactured by Sir William Siemens, the same German engineer who introduced electro-plating to Birmingham nearly sixty years earlier, and the engine was installed in the home of Lord Kelvin, the famous physicist, to provide him with electric lighting. Initially, the Clerk system was employed mainly in the larger types of gas engine. In 1891 he went on to introduce supercharging, substantially increasing an engine's power output by raising the pressure of the fuel feed pump.

The importance of Clerk's work was widely recognized, and his engine was awarded a Silver Medal at the Paris Exhibition in 1881, a Gold Medal at the 1882 Electrical Exhibition and a Gold Medal at the 1885 Inventions Exhibition held in London. In 1882, following the presentation of an erudite paper before the Institution of Civil Engineers, he was awarded the coveted James Watt Medal. In 1882 and again in 1886 he became the Institution's Telford

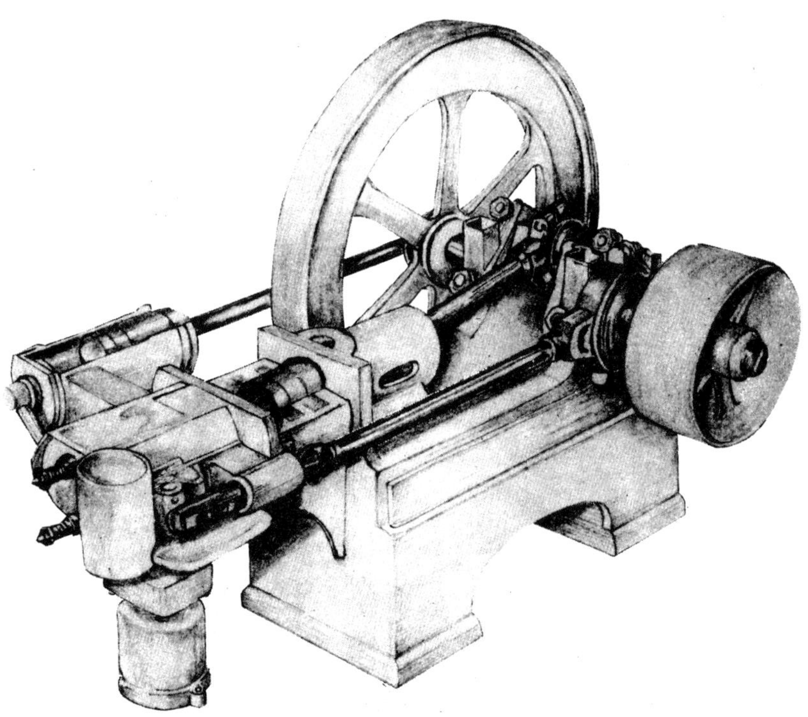

Clerk's patent two-stroke gas engine of 1881.

Prizeman. Dr Rudolph Diesel, the pioneer of the diesel engine, presented an important paper before the Institution of Mechanical Engineers in March 1912 and during the discussion he paid tribute to the pioneering work carried out by Clerk, acknowledging, 'The great merit of Mr Dugald Clerk's development of the two-cycle engine.' He told the meeting that following his own personal intervention in 1907 Dugald's original 1877 prototype engine had been placed in the German Museum of Masterpieces of Science and Technics in Munich. During 1886 Clerk published his first major book entitled *The Gas Engine*, which attained a large circulation and was reprinted in Germany, France and the United States. It remained a standard work for many years.

Dugald Clerk's work at Thomson Sterne's brought him increasingly into contact with Tangyes, who were already manufacturing a limited range of gas engines based upon developments of the original Lenoir design. Eventually, in 1885, he was persuaded to join the permanent staff at the Cornwall Works as Head of the Internal Combustion Engine Department. Before leaving his native Clydeside he married Margaret Hanney, daughter of Alexander

Hanney of Helensburgh, and she remained his devoted wife for forty-seven years. Events moved quickly at the Cornwall Works and within a year Tangyes were successfully selling a range of engines employing Clerk's Two-Stroke Cycle. Meanwhile, Dugald himself undertook further important research and development work.

The idea of compressing air alone into an engine cylinder and then injecting fuel in either a gaseous or liquid state was not new, and in 1887 Dugald Clerk built two experimental engines on the flame injection principle, igniting the gas by means of an external incandescent tube. Thermodynamically, his engines were similar to those built subsequently by the Yorkshire engineer, Herbert Akroyd Stuart and Dr Rudolph Diesel in the early 1890s, except that they relied upon compression for igniton, whereas Clerk required an external source. Akroyd Stuart had little business experience and no money and was compelled to sell his patents cheaply. The future of Tangyes, and indeed of a large section of British industry, might have been very different had Clerk anticipated Diesel's invention. Be that as it may, George Marks fully appreciated his colleague's brilliance. A great friendship and mutual respect developed between the two men while they were employed at Tangye's Cornwall Works.

Chapter 3
The Trio's Activities (1887–1893)

The day after presenting Mr George Tangye with his letter of resignation, George Marks went up to London and spent the night with his parents in Eltham. One can imagine their concern at the turn of events, for they were conservative and hated change, especially when it threatened the security of family life. Next day, he had meetings in the City with Worthington Pumps, well-known manufacturers of boiler feed water pumps, and with the American Elevator Company. Both readily agreed to grant him a sales agency for the Midland area. George and Maggie then departed for a short holiday, to help them gather their strength and quietly prepare for the future. George Marks's engagement with Tangye's officially ended on 21 July 1887, and the following week he put up his plate as a Consulting Engineer at 13 Temple Street, Birmingham. This was in the centre of the business quarter, only two minutes' walk from the Palladian-style church of St Philip's, which became the City's Cathedral.

During the next twenty years George Marks was involved with several important civil engineering works and with a variety of mechanical, hydraulic and electrical projects. He travelled extensively giving professional advice to both private undertakings and Governments. By hard work he steadily built up his reputation and gained wide recognition, but the financial rewards came slowly. It seems that this success was in part due to his extraordinary capacity for hard work, coupled with his professional integrity and enthusiasm for everything undertaken. His charming, kindly personality enabled him to make friends easily, and he enjoyed a remarkable ability for gaining people's confidence. His lifestyle was beyond reproach and he always appeared optimistic and pragmatic. He often declared, 'Whenever you combine theory with practice you find success.' Another of his favourite sayings was, 'Courage, the key to life.'

As an engineer, George Marks will be best remembered as the designer and builder of water-balance-operated cliff railways and steep incline tramways. He was responsible for the cliff railways built at Saltburn-by-the-Sea, Lynton & Lynmouth, Bridgnorth, Bristol, Aberystwyth and at Budapest in Hungary. He built, also, the steep incline tramway at Matlock in Derbyshire. Strictly speaking the first of the cliff railways at Saltburn was completed before George Marks became self-employed. The Lynton & Lynmouth project was commenced while he was still at the Cornwall Works, and his subsequent appointment as Consulting Engineer immediately after leaving Tangye's was natural because of his family connections with Lynton. All these projects are of considerable historical interest, as we shall see in the next chapter.

Initially, George concentrated upon his new sales agencies, which included an engineering insurance agency. He also undertook some enginering drawing work to help augment his income. He and Maggie sold their house in Lozells and took up residence in the Broad Street district, only ten minutes' walk from the office. Edward assisted him in his spare time with the preparation of drawings, many of which were commissioned to support patent applications. We learn from Edward Marks's journal that considerable time was devoted to a Mr Meacock's patent hydraulic valve. George Marks also accepted the appointment as architect to the new Soho Hill Infants School. Besides all these commitments, he sustained his interest in his church, and agreed to become Vice-President of the Soho Hill Mutual Improvement Society.

Edward Marks continued his employment in the Drawing Office at Tangye's Cornwall Works until September 1887. Whilst enjoying a short holiday with his parents in Eltham, he received by post the offer of a job as draughtsman at Young & Company's Ryland Street Works, in Birmingham's Gunsmiths' quarter. Tom and Henry Young were business acquaintances of George Marks, and manufactured a variety of lifting tackle and hydraulic machinery which Edward was now fully competent to handle. He was offered 30 shillings a week and promptly wired back his acceptance, taking up his new employment on 13 September, obviously pleased to get away from the unpleasant atmosphere then current at the Cornwall Works.

An entry in Edward's journal dated March 1888 made the first reference to a Miss Lily Houlton, living in Gillot Road, Edgbaston. Two months later he recorded, 'This evening I attended Spring Hill Baptist Chapel. Miss Houlton attends this chapel and I went up with the express desire of seeing her. I walked round to her lodgings with her and on the way told her that the affection I had for her was greater than that of a friend. It appeared to take her all by surprise, so that I left her to think it over.' Then as now, a young man's fancy was aroused, but things moved more slowly and more formally than is the custom today. Six days later Edward wrote to Lily Houlton, 'suggesting an interview'.

The following day, Maggie Marks called upon Lily Houlton and brought Edward a letter which he described as containing, 'All that I could desire.' Thereafter, the formality disappeared and Edward's journal made reference only to 'Lily'. She was a school teacher in the Ladywood district of Birmingham, and two years older than Edward. The younger daughter of the late Christmas Houlton, who came originally from Lowestoft, her widowed mother lived in Leopold Street, Derby. Their formal engagement was announced on Edward's twenty-second birthday, and lasted nearly five years. In the interval Edward worked hard and concentrated upon developing his career.

There can be little doubt that, from the moment of his own independence, George Marks hoped that his younger brother would eventually join him in business. In June 1888, upon George's advice, Edward left Youngs to join Ashwell & Company at the Victoria Foundry, Leicester, as General Manager, Engineering Department. Ashwell's manufactured fire extinguishers, pumps and hydraulic machinery. Maggie Marks once again came to Edward's assistance and trudged round the streets of Leicester until she found suitable accommodation for him in Flora Street, in the Black Friars district. George was convinced that the experience Edward could obtain from this appointment would be of great value to his own operations in future years.

Undoubtedly, Edward enjoyed his new job and found his social life in Leicester congenial. Through his attendance at the local Congregational Church, he established a close friendship with the Russell family, who traded as S. Russell & Son, Brassfounders. The friendship continued long after Edward returned to Birmingham, and many years later his eldest daughter, Gladys Ella, married Percy Russell, a Chartered Accountant. Whilst in Leicester, Edward continued to attend evening classes, and passed his examinations in astronomy, under the Cambridge University scheme. He returned to Birmingham at the weekends as often as possible to visit his fiancée,

George Croydon Marks, c. 1890.

Lily Houlton. On one such occasion, he and George attended a Liberal Party political meeting in the City, the first indication we have of the brothers' interest in the old Whig Party.

Near disaster befell the family in January 1889. George was taken critically ill with rheumatic fever, and for a few days there was grave concern about his survival. He was unable to attend to his business affairs for three months, and during this time Dugald Clerk came to the rescue. Clerk had left Tangye's a few weeks earlier with the intention of joining George as a full-time Consultant. Although no formal agreement was established between the two men, each apparently intended to pursue his own special interests, working from the same office. At the end of January, Maggie Marks and Edward had a meeting with Dugald Clerk in the Temple Street office to discuss the future of the business. Edward recorded in his journal, 'Mr Clerk seemed to think that he could manage things alright', which he undoubtedly did. Before George resumed work full-time, the whole Marks family attended Eltham Church for a service of thanksgiving for his complete recovery.

This early setback convinced George of the need to recruit his younger brother without delay. On 5 May he telegraphed Edward to come and see him as soon as possible, and his brother went to Birmingham that same evening. George proposed that Edward should join the business at 10 shillings a week, plus free board and lodging, a share of the profits from consultancy work, and in due course a partnership.

Edward appears to have inherited some of his father's caution, and was apprehensive about giving up his secure job at Ashwells. Naturally, at this time, his foremost need was a steady income to enable him to marry Lily as soon as possible. He wrote in his journal, 'Lily, Father, Mother, Emily and Addie' (note the order of listing), 'were all opposed to my accepting, but after much prayer and thought, I did so.' He worked a month's notice at Ashwells and in June 1889 joined his brother and Dugald Clerk in the Temple Street office.

The arrangement seems to have worked well, and exactly one year later, George confirmed in a letter to Edward that, henceforth, he would receive a salary of £104 per annum payable monthly, plus a fifth part of all profits after deduction of expenses arising from inspection work, the Worthington Pumps and American elevator sales agencies and insurance commissions. Edward was further required, 'To generally assist me in all my other work that may happen to require your services without additional remuneration.' It is important to note that Patent Agency work was expressly omitted.

The Chartered Institute of Patent Agents had been founded in 1882, and in June 1889, George Marks became formally registered as a Patent Agent under Rule 5. His letter confirming Edward's salary increase is the first clear indication we have that he was devoting a significant amount of his time to Patent Agency work. The original Register of Patents filed by Marks & Clerk has fortunately survived, revealing many well-known names, still remembered today as pioneers in their specialised fields. The first patent George Marks handled was No. 2742, filed in the early part of 1888 upon behalf of his brother's former employers, Tom and Henry Young, describing improvements in lifting-tackle. Others followed quickly, dealing with such diverse subjects as Hat Stretching Appliances, Brackets for Window Blinds, Mechanical Toys, Fishing Tackle and various apparatus developed by the old established Scale and Balance manufacturers, W. & T. Avery Ltd, who were later to occupy James Watts's famous Soho Foundry. One of the most interesting patents filed in 1888, was No. 9335, in the joint names of George Newnes, MP, George Croydon Marks and Bob Jones, the Lynton builder. The patent described the various unique features of the Lynton and Lynmouth Cliff Railway.

Patent Law as we know it today originates from the opening of the Great Exhibition of 1851, held in Hyde Park. There had been agitation for many years, calling for drastic reform of the law. This was brought to a head by the organizers of the Exhibition, led by Prince Albert, the Prince Consort, who for long had played an important rôle in the encouragement and promotion of enterprise in commerce and industry. The Patent Law Amendment Act of 1852 was the first Act on the Statute Book prescribing the procedure for obtaining patents for the protection of inventions. The new Act completely replaced the antiquated system that had existed for over three centuries, and separated Patents of Invention from other forms of Patent granted by Royal Prerogative, and placed them under the control of the Commissioners of Patents. The new Act provided for a single patent covering the whole of the United Kingdom, replacing the three separate patents previously necessary to ensure protection in England, Scotland and Ireland. Hitherto, it had been necessary to obtain protection in all three countries, each of which had its own procedures and fee structure.

Before 1852, all patent specifications were on parchment and enrolled in Chancery. Each carried the Great Seal in wax pendent at the foot. Largely as a result of the work of Bennet Woodcroft, FRS, the new Act required specifications to be printed on paper and published. The Commissioners of Patents became responsible for the provision of adequate indexes and other records, as well as a Register of Patents, all of which were to be made available to the public. The fees established by the Act, though sufficiently heavy in aggregate, were for the greater part payable at intervals after the sealing of the patent, and then only if the patentee wished to keep his patent in force for the full term.

However, the improvements and benefits arising from the 1852 Patent Law Amendment Act did not satisfy the Professional Institutions. Inventors, and those seeking information about their work, increasingly complained about 'The shocking lack of facilities afforded by the Patent Office', and resented the large profits made

The Great Seal of England attached to all patents of invention until 1883.

by the Government from patent fees amounting to over £60,000 annually. The Institution of Mechanical Engineers led the attack, submitting a memorial to the Lord Chancellor. Later, they were joined by the Institution of Civil Engineers, and together they brought great pressure to bear upon Sir John Romilly, the Master of the Rolls.

In 1883, the Patent Designs and Trade Marks Act abolished all vestiges of the pre-1852 practice, terminated the regime of the Commissioner of Patents, and set up the Patent Office as a Department of the Board of Trade. The Department was administered by the Controller General of Patents, Designs and Trade Marks, and survives substantially to this day. Under the new Act, the decision, deliberately taken by Parliament in 1852, to keep patent fees at a discouragingly high level was removed by the Board of Trade. Initially, the full term of a patent was 14 years, and this was increased to 16 years in 1919.

Following the 1883 Act there was a huge increase in the number of Patent applications made annually. One of the many important clauses of the Act stipulated that scientifically trained 'Examiners' should be appointed to the staff of the Patent Office to ensure that all new inventions were properly described in the specifications. No examination into the novelty of new applications was made until the official search was introduced in 1905, when the examining staff was increased five fold under the provisions of the Patents Act of 1902. The evolution of British Patent Law illustrates to a marked degree the peculiarly British practice of advancement by using and building on past experience, through a progression of small steps, in preference to sudden drastic changes of principle. Undoubtedly, the almost ponderous evolution of British Patent Law has very adequately protected many of the basic inventions which have contributed so greatly to our industrial strength.

It remains very much to George Marks's credit that, even while he was struggling to establish his independence as a Consulting Engineer, he fully appreciated the potential of Patent Agency work. Marks and Dugald Clerk both had the remarkable ability of dealing effectively and efficiently with a variety of projects simultaneously, and both mastered the complexities of Patent Law in an incredibly short time. Indeed, such was Marks's confidence in the subject, that he published a valuable little reference book in 1888, entitled, *The Inventor's Pocket Book.*

The list of well-known companies and distinguished inventors entrusting their patent applications to Marks & Clerk in the early years of the Partnership is too long to examine in any great detail. George Marks tended to attract Midland clients, whose inventions were mainly associated with methods of manufacture and improved products, whereas Dugald Clerk concentrated upon those pioneering new technology. Notable amongst Marks's early clients were J. S. Taylor and S. W. Challen, press manufacturers, whose works in Livery Street, Birmingham, produced many hundreds of large crank presses for the manufacture of sheet and hot metal pressings. In their heyday it would have been difficult to find a single metal-working factory in the Midlands without a Taylor & Challen press.

Another name appearing regularly in the Patent Register was that of Joseph Lucas, who established his lamp factory in Little King Street, Birmingham, in 1872. When the bicycle appeared on the roads he set to work and produced the 'King of the Road Cycle Hub Lamp', which burned oil. This was the beginning of the great Lucas motor components organization. In 1897, when the Company was incorporated and the 'horseless carriage' began to appear, oil gave way to acetylene, and acetylene, in its turn, to electricity. Lucas's original patents described mundane articles such as bicycle bells, pumps and valves for pneumatic tyres, and acetylene lamps. But by 1913, he had developed comparatively sophisticated electrical equipment for motor vehicles. Today, most British and many foreign cars employ Lucas components. The part this organization played in two World Wars was of incalculable value to the nation.

One of the many less well-known names appearing in the Register was that of H. J. Yates, who pioneered the modern gas-fired cooking appliance. In 1919 his company became a part of the Radiation Group. The resultant New World gas cooker produced by the associated firms was a technical landmark, for it introduced the Regulo variable thermostat control for the first time in cookers. Charles Winn, another early client, was a leading brassfounder in Birmingham. His Berkley Street Works manufactured industrial valves and fire-fighting equipment. The Chairman of R. W. Winfield & Company, W. R. Lane, appears in the Register. Winfield manufactured brass bedsteads, gas fittings, plumbers' brassfoundry and early electric light fittings in association with Colonel R. E. Crompton. In 1901, George Marks and W. R. Lane's wife, Janet, jointly patented a novel vegetable cutter. The celebrated Count von Zeppelin, who gave his name to the World War I German airship, employed Marks in 1907 to handle one of his patent registrations.

The other partner, Dugald Clerk, was named in over 100 patents, many of which were filed in association with the inventors of extremely important technological developments. The original Patent Register included at an early date such famous inventors' names as the Hon. C. A. Parsons, F. W. Lanchester, G. E. Bellis, A. Morcom and A. C. Pain of Bellis & Morcom Ltd, W. J. Crossley and J. Atkinson of Crossley Brothers, A. Cocking, W. E. Dickinson and E. Jones of Kynoch Ltd, S. Z. de Ferranti, and M. S. Napier.

The Hon. Charles Algernon Parsons perfected the steam turbine. The sixth and youngest son of an Irish peer, the Earl of Rosse, he was brought up in a scientific atmosphere. His grandfather had been a Vice-President of the Royal Society, and his father its President. Their home, Birr Castle, was for long a rendezvous for the leading scientists and engineers of the day. In 1873, Parsons went up to St John's College, Cambridge, to read mathematics. There he designed a high-speed epicycloidal steam engine. After graduation he moved to Sir W. G. Armstrong's Elswick Works in Newcastle-upon-Tyne, as a premium apprentice. Armstrong's management were so impressed with Parsons's inventive abilities, they allowed him to construct his epicycloidal engine. For a time it was coupled to a Siemens dynamo, supplying current for a powerful arc lamp on Elswick jetty. Although the engine performed remarkably well, the firm was not interested in undertaking its manufacture. Parsons then arranged for the engine to be sent to Easton & Anderson's works where his brother Clerc was employed. The Erith concern successfully produced several engines during the period of George Marks's employment, and there is little doubt that he made his first contacts with the Parsons brothers at this time.

Clerc Parsons later joined the famous locomotive builders, Kitsons of Leeds, who agreed to manufacture forty epicycloidal engines for driving dynamos. Upon completion of his four-year apprenticeship, Charles Parsons decided to join his brother in Leeds. He reached an agreement with Sir James Kitson, whereby he would set up an experimental shop in the works to develop naval torpedoes, agreeing to meet half the costs involved. In January 1883, at a critical stage in his work, Parsons married, but delayed his honeymoon in order to complete a series of tests in the nearby Roundhay Lake. Dutifully, his bride accompanied him each morning to the lakeside, but soon became seriously ill with rheumatic fever, and the project had to be abandoned. As soon as Katherine Parsons recovered, the young couple departed on an extended tour of the United States. On his return Parsons paid Kitsons his share of the costs of the experimental work on torpedoes, and looked around for new opportunities of continuing his development work on prime movers.

In January 1884, Parsons joined Clarke, Chapman & Company as a junior partner at their Gateshead Works, taking charge of the recently established Electrical Department. At that time the optimum speed of the dynamo was considerably greater than that of any reciprocating steam engine available, and many designers in the United Kingdom, Germany and the United States were trying to develop an efficient combination of the two. Charles Parsons concentrated on designing a steam turbine suitable for direct coupling to a dynamo. After only four months' work, and in spite of a whole range of new problems created by the phenomenally high rotational speeds of his turbine, he took out two patents describing his integral steam turbine and electric generator. These problems affected bearing design, lubrication, balancing and governing the speed of the turbine, with all of which he dealt satisfactorily. During the next four years, Clarke Chapman built 360 turbo-generators to Parsons's designs. Then, in June 1889, Parsons decided to dissolve the Partnership and established his own works on the north bank of the River Tyne.

Unfortunately, his original patents remained the property of Clarke Chapman, precluding him from further developing the axial-flow-type turbine. He discussed his problems with both George Marks and Dugald Clerk, and decided to concentrate on designing a turbine in which the flow of the steam was radial. During 1890, Marks & Clerk filed three extremely important patents upon his behalf. Patents Nos. 1120 and 14,994 described his modified turbine, and No. 11,083 covered methods of governing the speed of the turbine. In the following decade the Partnership filed many other patents in Parsons's name, describing the unique features of his designs, methods of manufacture, and their application to electricity generation and sea-going vessels. In 1894, Parsons was able to buy back his original patents from Clarke Chapman, and resumed his work developing the axial-flow-type turbine.

The story of Parsons's work and of his many remarkable achievements, especially his experiments with ship propulsion, requires a volume to itself. Here, it must suffice to say that no patents of comparable importance had been taken out in the field of prime movers, since James Watt patented his separate condenser in 1769. Mankind will ever be indebted to this most remarkable engineer, who died in February 1931, during a cruise to the West Indies.

The invention and early development of the internal combustion engine was the work of academics and highly specialized professional engineers, led by Dr Nicholas Otto, Dr Rudolph Diesel and Dugald Clerk. The majority of the subsequent improvements which made it a cheap, viable proposition were achieved by essentially practical men. Frederick William Lanchester was an exception, and his contribution to the design of the petrol engine and automobile was probably greater and more enduring than that of any other contemporary engineer. He came from a professional family background, and lived in Hove, where he received a good education. Later, he studied at the Normal College of Science in London, but after three years, largely for reasons of his own making, he failed to qualify. Instead of concentrating upon the work in hand, he spent his time studying the theory of flight, and patented a new slide rule cursor and an accelerometer.

Initially, he had some difficulty finding suitable employment, but in 1888, with the aid of an uncle, he secured a job with the Forward Gas Engine Company, a small but progressive company in Birmingham. At the age of 21 he was appointed Works Manager, and in the same year Marks & Clerk filed his patent No. 19,868, describing important improvements in gas engines. His work brought him into close contact with Dugald Clerk, and the two men became great friends. Further patent registrations followed in quick succession describing improved methods of engine governing, starting and ignition, which earned him over £3000 in royalties.

At this time, many eminent engineers misjudged the future course of events, believing that the prime mover of the future would be the gas engine. It gave a high thermal efficiency compared with the steam engine, the fuel was obtained from readily available small coal and other waste products comparatively cheaply; and petroleum products were still in their infancy, expensive and controlled by monopolies. Lanchester's future was poised between the motor car and the aeroplane, and his perspicacity convinced him that the petrol engine, as pioneered by Daimler and Benz in Germany, provided the logical answer to his motive power needs.

In spite of Lanchester's confidence that he could design a petrol engine sufficiently light to meet the demands of his proposed flying machine, his friend Dugald Clerk told him:

> 'Lanchester, you may be right, but you are a young man and must consider your reputation. If you were to put forward such a proposition seriously, you would be regarded as a crazy inventor, and your reputation as a sane engineer would be ruined.'

Accepting Dugald Clerk's advice, he set up his own company and devoted his energies to the development of the petrol engine and the motor-car. Concurrently with this work, he filed a patent entitled 'Aerial Machines', but this was ahead of its time and very largely ignored.

Lanchester's first experimental car was completed in 1896, and contained many of the essential features of the modern motor-car. Outstanding were its perfectly balanced and almost silent petrol engine, its torsionally rigid frame, dynamically stable steering, and epicyclic gearbox having direct drive for high speed. He employed his own patented design of magneto, valve gear and worm-and-wheel transmission gearing, eliminating for the first time the need for a chain drive to the road wheels. He undertook the design and building of special gear-cutting machinery, so necessary for the accurate manufacture of his gearbox and transmission components. A. B. Filson Young's classic, *The Complete Motorist*, first published in 1904, comments, 'There is probably no more interesting motor car from the engineer's point of view than the Lanchester. It is the outcome of extraordinary care and originality in design, and an extraordinary amount of deliberation and preparation. It is typical of the care with which this car has been designed, that it made its first public appearance at the Automobile Association's Richmond Trials in 1899, and secured the Gold Medal.'

Dugald Clerk became increasingly interested in the development of the motor-car and frequently advised and encouraged Lanchester. Both the newly founded Automobile Association and the Royal Automobile Club engaged Clerk as judge at several of their sponsored events, including the 1899 Richmond Trials, the 1900 Thousand Miles Trial, the 1901 Reliability Trials held in Glasgow and the 1903 Crystal Palace Event. Throughout the first twenty years' development of the motor-car, Clerk's advice was constantly sought by designers, manufacturers and trials organizers alike.

Unfortunately, space precludes the story of Lanchester's later life being told. Technically, he was unquestionably brilliant, but he was a difficult man, who didn't suffer fools gladly, and was unpopular with many of his contemporaries. He lacked commercial expertise and his company staggered on until overtaken by bankruptcy shortly before World War I. Later, Lanchester acted as a consultant to the Daimler Company, who continued to manufacture his cars. He wrote several books, including a book of verse, but money worries remained. He could not even afford to run his own car. 'It is an amazing experience', he wrote, 'to find that without any loss of faculties, the world has no use for me.' He died at his home in Birmingham in March 1946, aged seventy-eight.

Mention must be made of three more clients who entrusted Marks & Clerk with their patent work during the early formative years of the Partnership. George Bellis formed an association with Alfred Morcom in 1884, trading as G. E. Bellis & Company at Ledsam Street Works in the Ladywood district of Birmingham. Bellis had been apprenticed to Richard Bach, who is credited with building the first portable-type steam engine, the precursor of the traction engine. At the age of 28 Bellis established his own company, which eventually absorbed the Bach concern. Alfred Morcom had been Chief Engineer at the Sheerness Dockyard prior to joining Bellis, and in 1886 he recruited a young engineer, Albert Pain, whom he had known previously when working in Portsmouth Naval Dockyard. Pain became the company's Chief Draughtsman, and was responsible for several important inventions, probably the most important of which was a system of forced lubrication for use in totally enclosed high-speed steam engines, which he patented in 1891. By 1899, the Company required additional capital to finance its continued expansion, and it became publicly quoted on the Birmingham Stock Exchange, trading as Bellis & Morcom Ltd. Initially, they manufactured high-speed steam engines, having power outputs ranging from 5 to 2500 b.h.p. In 1905 they commenced the manufacture of spark ignition oil engines, later, in 1912, they produced the compression ignition diesel engine. They built submarine diesel engines in both World Wars, and undertook a major programme of reconditioning enemy submarine engines after World War I.

Francis and William Crossley established their works in the Openshaw district of Manchester in the early part of 1866, and since that date the company has been prominent in the development and manufacture of all types of internal combustion engine. Early production was based upon the Lenoir gas engine, and the Crossley brothers always claimed that their original gas engine was the first internal combustion engine produced in the United Kingdom. Later, they frequently consulted Dugald Clerk, and they were amongst the first British diesel engine manufacturers to introduce the scavenge pump two-stroke engine for locomotive, marine and industrial applications.

In 1888 former Prime Minister Neville Chamberlain's uncle, Arthur Chamberlain, effectively took control of Kynoch & Co. Ltd, Britain's second-largest ammunition factory. An unhappy state of affairs had existed in the company for some time. The business had made a loss in 1887, and an even greater loss was expected in 1888. The company's reputation and goodwill had been seriously damaged by the dubious behaviour of the founder, George Kynoch, and by its failure to ensure an acceptable standard of quality of its products. The factory at Witton, in the north-eastern suburbs of Birmingham, was passing through the most perilous period in its history, as one customer after another complained of defective cartridges. Chamberlain, known to be 'shrewd, stern and imperturbable', and his colleague, George Hookham, set about reorganizing the ailing company with the utmost urgency and vigour.

Having sorted out the unsatisfactory financial structure, by writing-off defective and obsolete items of stock, Chamberlain secured for the company its own brass rolling mill, and introduced new and meticulous inspection procedures. The development of the solid drawn brass cartridge case was probably George Kynoch's most strikingly successful contribution to improvements in ammunition in the last century, but the rolling mill which he leased from Muntz in 1877 was 'carried on by Mr Kynoch in his own name and for his own benefit'. Chamberlain purchased this mill for the company, and leased, with the option to buy, a second and larger mill in Lodge Road, in the Winson Green district of the city. He was able to tell shareholders at the 1890 Annual General Meeting that he had 'Already converted a heavy trading loss into a reasonably adequate profit', adding, 'your Directors are able not only to ensure a regular supply of metal at a fair price, but also generally to improve the quality of the rolling.'

In 1892, Chamberlain invited Dugald Clerk to join the Board as the Company's scientific adviser, responsible for the co-ordination of the several teams of specialists working on the development of new machinery for ammunition production, and on new nitro-glycerine-based explosives for the mining and civil engineering industries. In 1893 Dugald Clerk undertook important pioneering work on the design of steel shells, and was associated with other Kynoch employees in patents describing improved types of machinery and methods of manufacture. E. Jones headed the team responsible for improvements at the rolling mills; E. B. Dickinson concentrated upon a diversity of new products, including fog signal detonators for use on the railways. Important work in the field of new explosives for blasting became the responsibility of A. J. Cocking, a brilliant young scientist discovered by Arthur Chamberlain. The work of these men under the leadership of Chamberlain and Hookham successfully guided the fortunes of the Witton works for nearly a quarter of a century.

The progress of the successful, both individuals and corporate bodies, usually proceeds at a steady measured pace for a period, and then, often from necessity, takes a bold step forward in order to maintain its momentum. The Marks & Clerk partnership took several such steps in the years 1892–93. After his recovery from rheumatic fever in 1889, George Marks consolidated his position as both a Consulting Engineer and Patent Agent, and his brother Edward proved to be an admirable and competent assistant. Both had improved their professional status by gaining full membership of the Institution of Mechanical Engineers and of the Chartered Institute of Patent Agents. George also became an Associated Member of the Institute of Civil Engineers in recognition of his work on cliff railways. During the same period, Dugald Clerk widened his spheres of influence and responsibility. He was now known all over the industrial world for his work developing the internal combustion engine and the use of gaseous fuels. He had become widely recognized as an expert witness in technical and scientific matters, and his services were constantly sought on both sides of the Atlantic. In addition to his work at Kynoch's he was also appointed consultant to the Patent Shaft & Axletree Co. Ltd, another old-established and well-respected West Midlands engineering company controlled by the wealthy Docker family through their Metropolitan Carriage, Wagon & Finance holding company.

The original Partnership Patent Register lists the names of several important clients located in the North West of England. Rapid developments in textile machinery were taking place at this time and several leading manufacturers of locomotives, internal combustion engines and electrical machinery had already established their works in the Manchester area. In 1892, the partners decided to open a branch office at 6 Victoria Station Approach, in the centre of Manchester, providing the first link in a chain of branch offices which eventually became worldwide. Eighteen months later they took another major step forwards by deciding to extend their operations to London. In September 1893, they took a lease on office premises at 5 Furnivals' Inn, in Holborn. Within a few months these were found to be too small, and larger premises were acquired at 18 Southampton Buildings in Chancery Lane, both addresses being conveniently adjacent to the Patent Office. Next, both George Marks and Dugald Clerk decided to move their offices permanently to Southampton Buildings, thereby shifting the firm's centre of gravity to London, leaving Edward Marks in charge of the Birmingham and Manchester offices.

The other major step forward taken by the Partners in 1893 was an extension of their publishing activities. George Marks, as already noted, published his first book in 1888. His second, entitled *Hydraulic Machinery*, followed in 1891. Edward had three books to his credit. His *Notes on the Construction of Cranes & Lifting Machines* appeared in 1892, and *Engineering Materials* and *Notes on the Construction & Working of Pumps* were published in the following year. All were produced by the Technical Publishing Company, whose offices were in Chancery Lane, London. Soon after their removal to London the Partners launched a new weekly periodical called *The Practical Engineer*, which was also produced by Technical Publishing.

Looking back, one wonders how George Marks and Dugald Clerk found sufficient hours in the day to cope with so much activity, for all the evidence indicates that they employed a very small staff. The completion and formal opening of the Clifton Rocks Cliff Railway in Bristol and the Matlock Tramway also took place in 1893. Both had been very demanding on George and Edward Marks's time during construction. But, for Edward, the real climax of the year came on 29 June 1893, when his marriage to Lily Houlton took place at the Normanton Road Congregational Church in Derby. The service was conducted jointly by the local minister and the Marks's family friend, the Rev. Charles Lemoine, from Soho Hill in Birmingham. After a short honeymoon, the couple returned to Edgbaston, where they lived for the next thirty-five years.

Chapter 4
Cliff Railways and Steep
Incline Tramways

In 1830, a Mr Hugill presented an address to the people of Whitby and its vicinity, proposing the extension of the commerce of the area by constructing a railway across the Yorkshire Moors to Pickering and Malton. Five years on, James Falshaw, later Sir James, the distinguished Chairman of the North British Railway, was employed by Hamar & Pratt to supervise the construction of a horse-drawn railway from Whitby to Pickering. The gradients on the line proved too steep for horse traction and the expediency of using fully laden descending water-tanks was employed to haul up the loaded coaches. The tanks were emptied at the foot of the incline, and in their turn were hauled back to the top by the now heavier descending coaches. The first cliff railway to be constructed in the United Kingdom was built at Scarborough forty years later and employed the same water balance principle. It seems probable that the then already defunct Whitby railway provided the inspiration for the scheme which was promoted by a local hotel owner.

Scarborough became a popular spa in the 1870s, and was one of the first coastal resorts to offer visitors the facility of beach bathing-machines. Several smart new hotels were built on the cliff top, and the town became a great favourite with people living in the Yorkshire industrial towns. It enjoyed a good rail link with York and beyond, and it soon became the principal resort on the North East coast to cater for the new British custom of an annual family holiday by the seaside. Its promoters realized that there was a need to improve the access to the beach by removing the fatigue of climbing the cliffs, and the South Cliff Tramway Company was formed. A Mr Jousey was appointed architect, and local contractors, Stewart & Bury, laid the 4 ft 8½ in. standard-gauge line to a gradient of 1 in 1.75 at a cost of £8000. The line opened on 6 July 1876, was 284 ft long, and ran from a point on the foreshore, adjacent to the Spa, to the Esplanade, passing through the colourful South Cliff gardens. The water balance principle was used, whereby water tanks were built into the underframes of the two passenger cars. The tank under the car at the upper platform was filled with water, and the tank under the car at the lower platform was emptied, allowing the heavier weighted upper car to descend the incline, causing the lighter cable connected lower car to ascend. The position was then reversed. Two Crossley gas engines were employed to pump sea water to the top of the cliff, and the water discharge from the car tanks at the lower station was returned to the sea.

The scheme proved an immediate success, and a second installation known as the Central Tramway was opened in August 1881. This was 234 ft long at a gradient of 1 in 2, and ran from Foreshore Road to the top of St Nicholas Cliff. The water pumps were driven by a pair of steam engines manufactured by John Fowler & Company of Leeds, and the cliff top pulley around which the cable connecting the two cars passed, incorporated Fowler's Patent Clip Drum arrangement. Developed originally for use with steam cultivating machinery, the Clip Drum ensured that the cable was at all times tightly gripped by a series of clamps arranged around the periphery of the drum. This made the haulage system more positive and safer than the simple pulley arrangement employed on the original South Cliff railway. Although best known as a manufacturer of ploughing engines and railway locomotives, Fowler supplied the steam engines and other machinery for the first funicular railway on the slopes of Mount Vesuvius in Italy in 1879. This project inspired the well-known Neapolitan folksong, 'Funiculi Funicula'. Later, in 1899, Fowler built the massive funicular which descended into the Great Rift Valley in East Africa. This was ordered by the British Government during the great race to gain rail access to Lake Victoria ahead of the Germans' drive inland from Dar-es-Salaam.

The immediate interest aroused by the Scarborough cliff railways encouraged other resorts to propose similar schemes. In the period 1880–82, Tangye's received several enquiries for water balance machinery, and it is directly as a result of these that George Marks became personally interested in cliff railways.

Tangye received an order from the Middlesborough Estate Ltd, owners of the Saltburn Improvement Society in 1883, for the supply of a gas engine, water pump and other items of machinery for a water-balance-operated cliff railway being built by the Society at Saltburn-by-the-Sea, in North Yorkshire. The extent of Tangye's contribution to the overall design is not clear, but several Birmingham firms were involved as sub-contractors, indicating that their influence probably went beyond the supply of the engine and pump. The two passenger cars were built by the Metropolitan Carriage Works in Saltley, and the haulage rope came from Latch & Batchelor Ltd, both well-established Birmingham companies. George Marks is known to have made several visits to Saltburn whilst the railway was under construction.

The railway was opened to the public on Whit Monday, 2 June 1884, and operated from the Lower Promenade, opposite the Pier, to the Marine Parade on top of the cliff. Rising 114 ft at a gradient of 1 in 1.33, the 207 ft long railway was originally built to a 3 ft 9 in. gauge, but in 1921 this was altered to the 4 ft 8½ in. standard gauge. In all other respects, the system operates today very much as it was built, except that the gas engine has been replaced by electric motors fed direct from the mains supply.

A remarkable Quaker family were responsible for the development of Saltburn as a resort. The Pease family of Darlington were influential merchants and bankers who came into prominence as the promoters of the Stockton & Darlington Railway, the world's first steam-hauled public railway. Edward Pease (1767–1858), the head of the family at the time, was a 'Plain' Quaker of the old school and appointed George Stephenson as Engineer to the line on the very day the Royal Assent was given to the Act authorizing its construction. Edward's second son, Joseph (1799–1872), drafted the original Prospectus for the Company when only 19 years of age, and devoted much of his life to the railways and heavy engineering industries of the North East. He was the first Quaker to be elected a Member of Parliament, and married Emma Gurney, daughter of the wealthy Norwich Quaker banking family. In 1829, Joseph Pease and his brother-in-law, Francis Gibson, purchased 500 acres of land called Middlesborough and built a new port on the site. They received financial support from the famous bankers, Nathan Rothschild and Moses Montefiore, and within a few years prospered greatly as new heavy industries became established in the area. The flourishing new town of Middlesborough resulted from their enterprise.

In later life, Joseph built a house called 'Cliff House' in the North Yorkshire Parish of Marske, which included the small fishing hamlet of Saltburn. Each year it was customary for the whole family

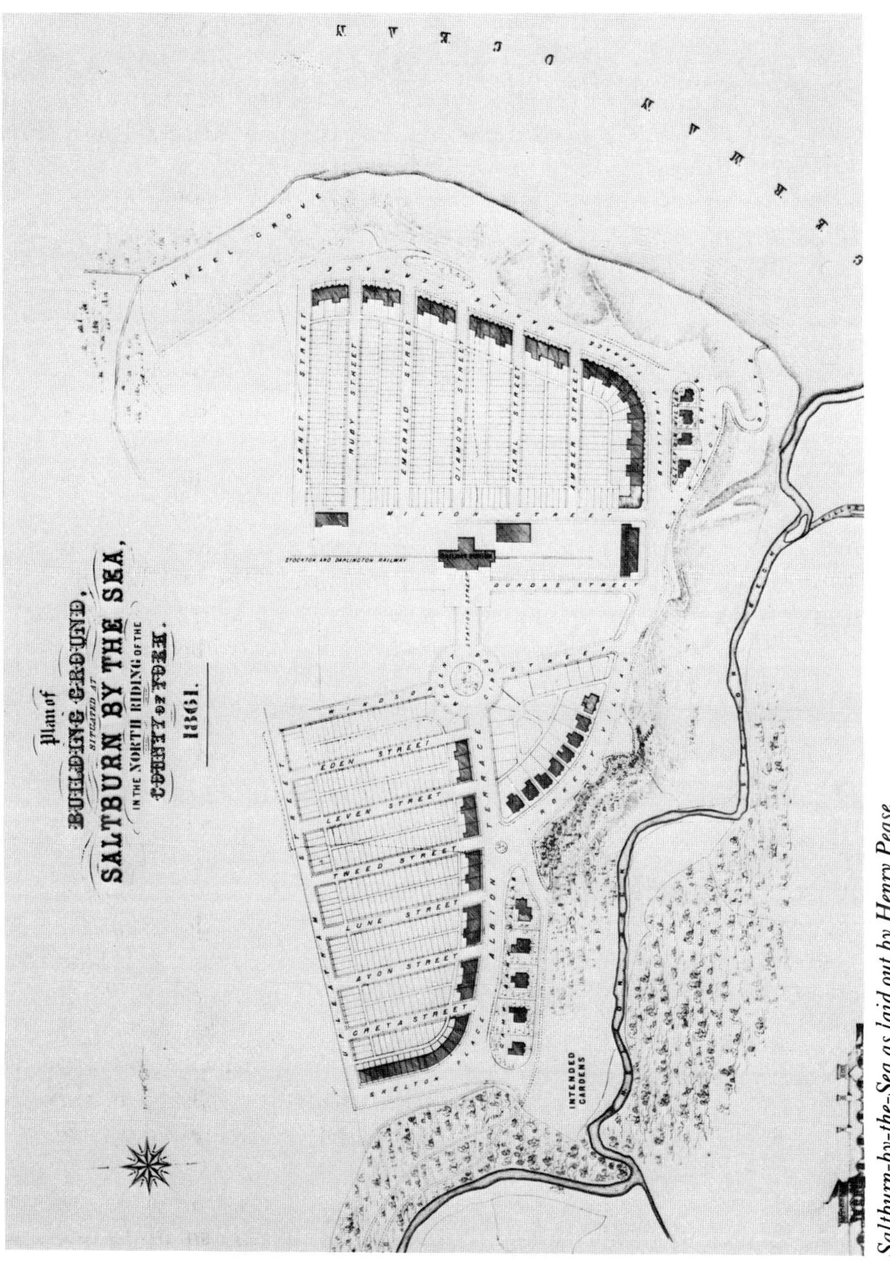

Saltburn-by-the-Sea as laid out by Henry Pease.

to spend part of the summer at 'Cliff House' and its adjoining cottages. Joseph's younger brother, Henry Pease (1807–81), the dreamer and philosopher in the family, derived enormous pleasure from these visits, and in due course had a vision of a 'New Jerusalem' built on the cliffs at Saltburn for the benefit and well-being of the local industrial workers and their families. Land was purchased from the Earl of Zetland, and a new Company, The Saltburn Improvement Society, was formed with Henry Pease as its Chairman. Other Directors included Isaac Wilson and William Hopkins, proprietors of the successful Quaker engineering company, Gilks, Wilson & Hopkins Ltd, together with William Cudworth, shipbuilder, Engineer to the Stockton & Darlington Railway and builder of much of the port of Middlesborough. By 1861, the dream had begun to take shape. The railway was extended from adjoining Redcar, to a new terminus at Saltburn, the palatial Zetland Hotel and a new Convalescent Home were completed, and Henry Pease built himself a fine town house in Britannia Terrace. Other streets quickly followed, the 'Jewel Streets of the New Jerusalem' – Amber, Pearl, Diamond, Emerald, Ruby and Coral Streets sprang up in white brickwork. In 1869, the pier and a somewhat crude-looking vertical lift to the top of the 100-ft high cliffs were completed, although the latter was demolished in 1883 to make way for the new water balance railway.

Shortly before Henry's death in 1881, the Improvement Society got into financial difficulties and was rescued by the Middlesborough Estate Company, who acquired all the Society's property and assets. Many years later, Joseph's grandson, Sir Alfred Pease, MP, wrote, 'The Improvement Society adopted white bricks when building Saltburn for the realization of their dreams of a celestial city. My grandfather, who had become blind and had to judge by the description of others for their loveliness and suitability, used them for constructing many Public Buildings in Darlington. The result was that a great number of cold looking streets came into existence when, had other material been used, a warmer looking a more attractive town might have come into being.' With obvious sadness, he concluded his recollections, 'We have all to accept the fact that with an enormous increase in population, there must be less of God's world and more of man's mark upon it.'

On 13 April 1887, Edward Marks recorded in his journal that his brother George had that day returned to Birmingham following a

Saltburn-by-the-Sea cliff railway from the pier.

visit to Lynton to see his mother's kinsman, Bob Jones. Three days later he recorded that he had been assisting George since his return from Devonshire, with the preparation of drawings to support the Lynton hydraulic lift patent application. This is obviously a reference to patent No. 9535, which was subsequently filed on 30 June 1888.

It is not clear whether George discussed the proposed cliff railway with Bob Jones as Tangye's accredited representative, or simply as a private individual. In either event it seems that his visit had Tangye's full approval, for the subsequent design work undertaken during George's last three months' employment at the

The Saltburn cliff railway as operating in 1985.

Cornwall Works was carried out in the firm's Drawing Office. Shortly after George put up his plate as a Consulting Engineer, Bob Jones visited Birmingham in order to discuss the future of the project and to clarify their working relationship.

During the April 1887 visit to Lynton, which had involved a long and tedious train journey to Barnstaple, and a final 20 miles by private carriage over the North Devon hills, George Marks met a gentleman who was to have a profound influence upon the remainder of his life. George Newnes, the immensely wealthy founder of the popular newspaper *Tit Bits*, recently elected Member of Parliament for Newmarket, and his wife, were staying in Lynton with their friends, Sir Thomas and Lady Hewitt. In later life, when created Baronet, Sir George Newnes left biographical notes describing the sequence of events which brought the two men together. Although somewhat apocryphal when describing the technical innovations involved, and the time taken to fulfil his dream, they indicated the habitual eagerness and dynamic character of the man.

He recorded how he and his wife had become absolutely charmed by the beauty of Lynton and the surrounding countryside, and how

... From Below

their pleasure was spoilt only by the sight of horses struggling to cope with the traffic of the district. He had a perfect horror of cruelty to any living thing, especially creatures so helpless as an animal in the service of man. He recorded his displeasure with the long drive from Barnstaple to Lynton, in spite of the fact that his host provided extra horses to draw the carriages up the last steep hill to his house.

One day at a suitable moment, George Newnes tackled his host, asking, 'Has it ever occurred to you that the River Lyn, which rolls down like a torrent, might be harnessed, and made to bring up every ton of coal and every passenger from Lynmouth to Lynton, without any cruelty to the poor labouring beasts, and any danger to human life?'

'Yes,' replied Sir Thomas, 'the idea of a lift or railway has often been considered, but for one reason or another, it has never been definitely taken up.' Whereupon, Newnes then outlined the principle of the water-balance cliff railways operating at Scarborough and Saltburn.

'Is there anyone in this place who is likely to undertake the construction of such a railway?' enquired the visitor. After only a

Lynton & Lynmouth cliff railway with Sir George Newnes and Bob Jones on the platform.

moment's thought, Sir Thomas despatched a messenger to summon Bob Jones to join them after dinner that very night.

'That night we fixed up a plan by which we could make a cliff railway. I took the rest in hand, and in a month the work was begun,' recorded Newnes with his characteristic pragmatism.

A new company, The Lynmouth & Lynton Lift Company, was formed with George Newnes as its Chairman. He undertook the provision of adequate finance and attended to the legal matters necessary to obtain Parliamentary authority for the use of the waters of the River Lyn. Bob Jones and George Marks concentrated upon the design and construction of the railway. The trackbed was excavated out of the hard limestone rock forming the cliff, to a depth sufficient to allow the passenger cars to pass under bridges which had to be constructed where the line interfered with existing paths and roadways. Retaining walls were built either side of the trackbed, and the lime for the mortar used was obtained from kilns built at the foot of the cliff. The length of the line was 890 ft, the longest of any of Britain's cliff railways, laid to a gradient of 1 in 1.8, and giving a vertical rise of 490 ft from Lynmouth Esplanade to Lee Road, Lynton. Flat-bottomed steel rails were laid to a gauge of 3 ft 8 in. and fastened to larch sleepers bolted directly to the rock face by fang-bolts at 6 ft centres. Two lines of railway were provided, one for each car. The inner rails of each line were spaced only 8 in. apart in order to minimise the amount of excavation required, except at the mid-point beneath the North Walk, where the gap was widened sufficiently to allow the cars to pass each other.

The water for operating the counter balance was drawn from the river at Lynbridge and conveyed through 6-in. diameter iron pipes laid under the roadway to a reservoir provided near the upper end of the railway. A system of valves allowed the 700 gallons capacity water-tanks mounted in the car under-frame to be filled quickly when at the summit station, and upon reaching the bottom, the water was discharged through a conduit into the sea. The advantage of the water balance system over the constant haulage alternative, was that the amount of water used in the descending car tanks could be varied according to the need. If more passengers were being carried down than were to be taken up, the amount of water required was obviously less than if the position were reversed. A system of electrical signalling was introduced so that the amount of water supplied to the descending car tank was related to the

Lynton & Lynmouth cliff railway car.

number of ascending passengers, ensuring the minimum amount of water wastage.

The locally made passenger car bodies were detachable from the under-frames and provided with wheels which permitted them to be easily run-off on to either the upper or lower station platforms, when it was desired to carry goods vehicles or other merchandise. Initially it is said that the railway made more ascents carrying goods than foot passengers. In the early 1900s it was frequently used for transporting motor-cars, which would otherwise have had extreme difficulty negotiating the steep roadways in the district. Each car body was arranged to seat twenty passengers seated longitudinally facing each other. The cars were connected by two 7/8 in. diameter Lang's-lay steel haulage ropes, each having a breaking strain of 27 tons, passing over a double grooved pulley at the top of the incline. Balancing tail ropes were fitted to each car, passing over another grooved pulley at the bottom of the incline,

... From Below

these ropes having the effect of steadying the cars when in motion.

In later years, both Sir George Newnes and Bob Jones individually claimed the credit for the design of the railway, but the connoisseur will have no difficulty discerning the hand of the professional engineer in the mechanical details of the system. George Marks never claimed any credit for the original bold idea of the railway, but with every justification he must be recognized as the engineer who gave the project substance, and as the designer who perfected the several unique safety features, which have withstood the test of over ninety years' almost continuous summer working without mishap or injury.

The unique safety features were the subject of patent No. 9535 filed in June 1888 in the joint names of Sir George Newnes, Bob Jones and George Marks. Four separate systems for braking the cars were described, any of which could be applied to either car, independently of the other. The first came into operation in the event of the haulage ropes breaking, or becoming in any way deranged, and automatically applied steel wedges to both sides of the running rail, stopping the cars instantly. The second was a manually operated emergency brake, operated by the conductor from the car platform, applying similar steel wedges to the running rails. Thirdly, the speed of the cars was controlled by a centrifugal governor driven by the car axle. Any undue increase in speed caused slippers to be applied automatically to the top of the rails, immediately slowing down the rate of descent. The fourth option comprised an ingenious and powerful hydraulically operated braking system under the direct control of the conductor. This system controlled the actual movement of the cars once the water-tank in the car at the bottom of the incline had been emptied. Each car was provided with two accumulators powered by variable stroke eccentric driven pumps driven from the car axle. The accumulator rams were loaded by a suspended weight, which itself was linked by a chain and sprocket wheel to a pedestal-mounted handwheel operated by the conductor. The combination of the weight multiplied by the purchase in the gearing produced a pressure of 1000 p.s.i. The action of the falling weight upon the accumulator ram kept the water pressure in the four brake cylinders constant, but when greater pressure was required, the conductor turned the handwheel, depressing the ram further, and thereby applying additional pressure to the column of water in the accumulator causing the cars to stop. When it was desired to travel normally and to prevent the brakes gripping the running rails, the conductor turned the handwheel in the opposite direction, raising the ram sufficiently to allow the water in the accumulator to discharge through ports in the upper end of the cylinder, and thereby overcoming the effects of the suspended weight.

It will be understood that with the pressure pumps constantly at work to keep the brake cylinders charged, the normal tendency of the mechanism was to maintain the brakes always thrusting against the rails, and that it was the duty of the conductor to prevent the cars stopping by keeping the pressure off when they were in motion. The brakes on each side of the cars were entirely independent of each other, although both were connected to and controlled by the single conductor's handwheel. Furthermore, the individual brakes were of such power that any application to one car immediately arrested the movement of both. Undoubtedly the most far-sighted

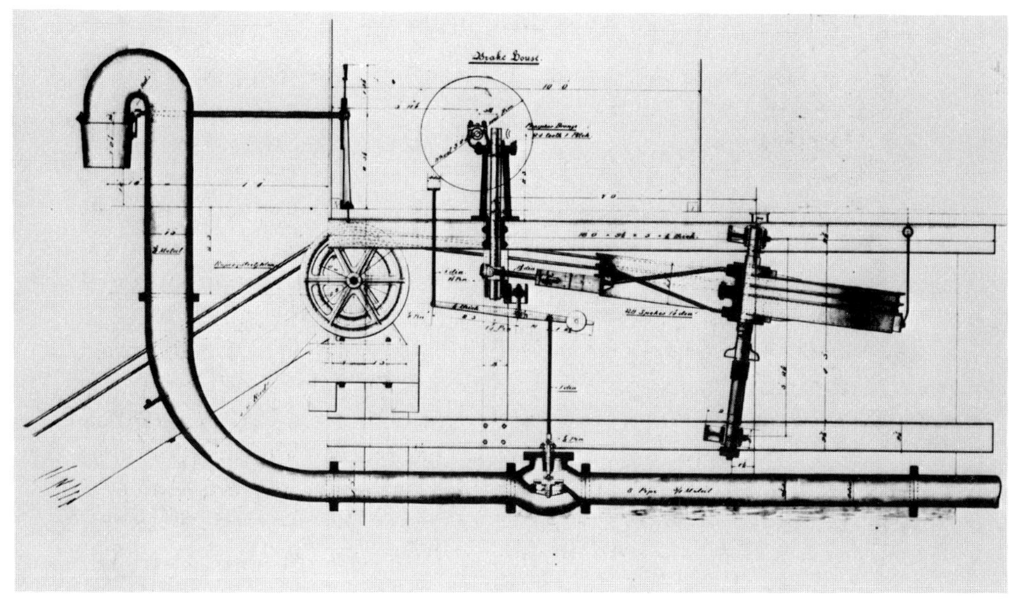

Saltburn cliff railway brake gear.

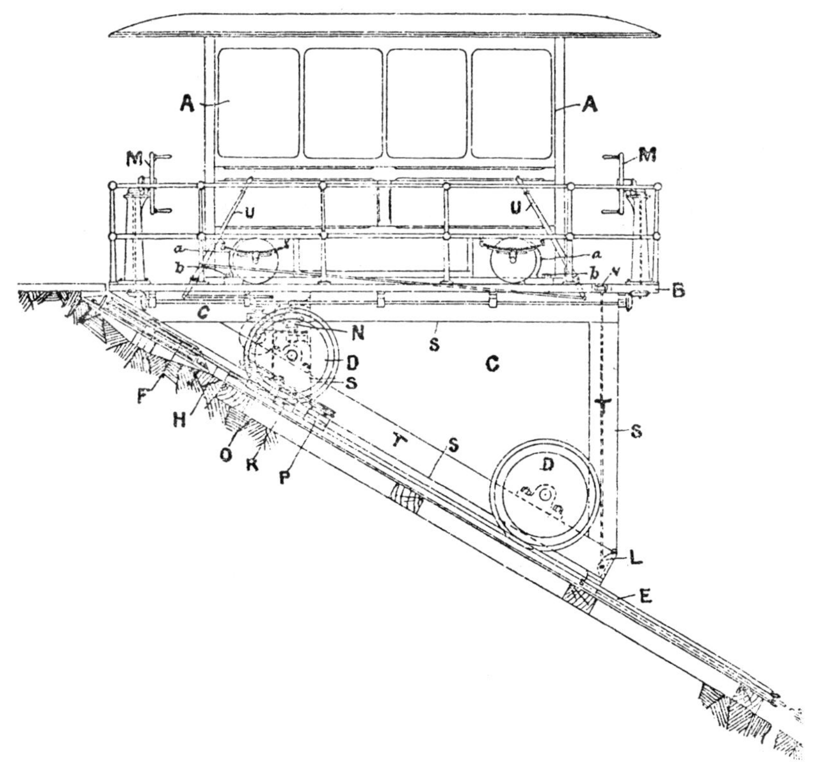

*Drawing attached to patent specification No. 9535 of 1888 depicting the Lynton &
Lynmouth car.*

Lynton & Lynmouth cliff railway transporting an early motor-car – c. 1904.

feature of the design was that in the event of the conductor accidentally or carelessly releasing his hold on the handwheel, pressure was immediately restored to the brake cylinders, and the cars were stopped. This arrangement was the precursor of the modern 'Dead-man's Handle', incorporated in the controls of all present-day diesel and electric locomotives.

The public opening of the railway took place on Easter Monday,

7 April 1890, in the presence of many local dignitaries and a large gathering of the press corps, who had travelled down from London at Sir George Newnes's invitation. The ceremony was performed by Mrs Jeune, the Lady of the Manor, and was followed by a traditional celebration luncheon at the Valley Rocks Hotel in Lynton.

The completion of the cliff railway was the first link in the chain which bound George Newnes permanently to Lynton. Soon after the opening ceremony he began to occupy himself with thoughts of building a country house in the area, where his family and friends could come for relaxation. In due course, he purchased Hollerday Hill, above Lynton, and transformed the hillside into an area of exceptional beauty. In later years, he derived great satisfaction from sharing his enjoyment with visitors to the twin villages, by opening the grounds to the general public every day except Sundays. The spell which this place cast over him from the very beginning was never broken.

In 1895, George Newnes was instrumental in obtaining an Act of Incorporation, authorizing the building of a narrow gauge railway from Barnstaple to Lynton, passing through some of the most exquisite hill scenery in the British Isles. He loved the challenge of local transport problems for their own sake, and provided most of the capital required for the construction of the 19.5 miles long, 1 ft 11 in. gauge system. The 1000 ft summit of the line was at Wood Bay and included a handsome viaduct at Chelfham over the River Yeo. The line was formally opened by Lady Newnes at a splendid ceremony held on 11 May 1898. Subsequently, due to Sir George's foresight and initiative, the railway became the first in Great Britain to have an associated motor omnibus feeder service. Shortly after World War I, the Company was taken over by the London & South Western Railway, which itself became a part of the Southern Railway in the 1923 Grouping. Regular services were operated until 1935, when the line was closed and the track lifted.

George Newnes was created a Baronet in 1895, and that year he announced his intention of donating a fine new town hall to the people of Lynton. Built by Bob Jones, it was officially opened in 1900 and stands today as a splendid example of Victorian architecture and craftsmanship, embodying local stone and the best of English timber. Always a benefactor of the Congregational Church, he made a substantial contribution towards the cost of a new church in Lynton, which Bob Jones was commissioned to build near the town hall. Another benefit which he had hoped to confer upon the district, was the building of a new pier at Lynmouth. He introduced a Bill before Parliament, and paid all the expenses associated with the passing of the Bill, but failing health prevented him proceeding with the project. Sadly, he died in June 1910, at the comparatively early age of 59, and was buried in his beloved Lynton. His generosity was not confined to the people of Lynton and Lynmouth, and in 1897, in order to mark the Queen's Diamond Jubilee, he presented the London Borough of Putney, where he had his London residence, with a fine new public library.

There is little doubt that from the moment of their first meeting in April 1887, George Marks and George Newnes established a great mutual respect and friendship for each other. Both men had similar religious and political backgrounds; both had entrepreneurial attitudes to business and were extremely hard working; and both shared common interests in mechanical innovation and technical publishing. During the next two decades the relationship became mutually beneficial and profitable, and each was able to give the other valuable assistance in a variety of ways. Undoubtedly, George Marks's decision to stand for Parliament in 1906 was influenced by his friendship with Newnes. Equally, Newnes's wide-ranging business contacts were of great benefit to Marks during the formative years of the Marks & Clerk Partnership. In addition to his own very successful printing and publishing activities, which included George Newnes Ltd, Newnes & Pearson Printing, *Country Life*, and the *Westminster Gazette*, Newnes was invited to join the board of C. A. Parsons Ltd. No doubt, this appointment stemmed originally from George Marks's long-standing connection with the Hon. Charles Parsons.

The immediate success of the Lynton & Lynmouth Cliff Railway encouraged the two men to look elsewhere for suitable sites for other cliff railways, where they could employ the technology they had developed and patented in 1888. Already, they were facing competition from a London firm, R. Waygood & Co, who had built a cliff railway operating on the water balance principle at Folkestone in Kent in 1885. Later, this company became incorporated as the well-known lift manufacturers, Waygood-Otis Ltd, and supplied the hundreds of escalators and lifts used in London's underground railway system. In 1891, Newnes and Marks finalized two new projects on which they had been engaged for some time. The first, in the Avon Gorge at Bristol, adjacent to Brunel's beautiful suspension bridge, and the second on the banks of the River Severn, at the Shropshire market town of Bridgnorth.

The beginnings of Marks's involvement with the Clifton Spa development seem to stem from a visit George and Maggie made to old friends, the Belsher family in Bristol, in October 1887. It is unlikely George would have made such a visit so soon after setting up on his own, unless there were also some business prospects linked with the visit. A few months later he was formally appointed Engineer to the project, responsible for the design of the railway, the Spa pump room and the Clifton Hydro. Initially, there appears to have been some difficulty arranging the necessary finance, and the commencement of work was delayed until George Newnes took a personal interest in the scheme enabling construction work to start on 7 March 1891.

The railway ran from Hotwells Road for a distance of 450 ft to the top of Zion Hill on the Gloucester side of the river. Four tracks were provided and the whole length of the line was in a tunnel 28 ft wide, having a height of 17 ft at its crown. It was laid at a gradient of 1 in 2.5, giving a vertical rise of 200 ft. The tunnel was cut out of solid limestone rock, but unforeseen difficulties were soon encountered with the rock strata, which precluded, for safety reasons, the use of machine drilling equipment. The faults prevented one gang of men from working above another in the usual manner when removing the rock, and it was found necessary to brick-line the tunnel from end to end. These difficulties not only considerably delayed the completion of the project, but increased the original estimated cost from £10,000 to a figure in excess of £30,000. The formal public opening took place on 11 March 1893.

The mechanical arrangements were similar in every respect to those used at Lynton and Lynmouth. The employment of four cars, each on its own track, necessitated two sets of rope pulleys at the summit, and Marks decided to add yet another set of hand-operated brakes to the system, which operated directly on the summit pulley sheaves. These brakes were controlled from a central cabin at the summit, which also controlled the supply of water to the descending cars, and Marks rather strangely described his decision to incorporate this additional safety feature as a 'Sentimental reason'. Their incorporation meant that at any moment, three men, the two

Clifton Rocks, Bristol, cliff railway, illustrating the four railway tracks.

conductors on the cars, and the controller in the summit cabin, individually, had the means of stopping the motion of each pair of cars at will. A reservoir was arranged near the summit station for filling the car tanks, and when the cars had completed their descent, the water was discharged into the bottom reservoir, which was provided with a duplicate set of Otto four-stroke gas engines and pumps for returning the water to the upper reservoir. The engine room, waiting-rooms and track were all formed in the limestone rock.

The capacity and general adequacy of the system was soon put to the test, for in the days following the official opening as many as 1000 passengers an hour were carried. During the first six months of operations, some 330,400 people passed through the turnstiles, and in May 1894 it was decided to separate the cliff railway from the other activities of the Clifton Spa development. A new limited liability company was formed in which George Newnes retained the whole of the share capital. In December 1894, the local *Bristol Magpie* published a brief monograph praising George Marks, and describing him as a man of medium height, possessed of dark hair and deep-set eyes, adding, 'Mr George Croydon Marks takes the greatest interest in the management of the Spa concerts, and personally superintends the intricate details of the elaborate baths nearing completion. He is head and shoulders above his fellows in the profession, and is extremely genial to those who enjoy his acquaintance' – praise indeed.

The railway was purchased by the Bristol Tramways & Carriage Company in 1912, and continued to prosper until the Bristol Port & Pier Railway closed its Hotwells station in 1922. This caused a steady decline in traffic on the cliff railway, which eventually closed in September 1934. But that is not the end of the story. On the outbreak of war in 1939, plans were made for the BBC to operate from Bristol in the event of heavy air attacks on London. It was realized, however, that these attacks might well extend to Bristol, and a search was made for a suitable underground headquarters in the area. Eventually, the authorities decided that the disused tunnel on the Hotwells branch of the Great Western Railway was suitable for this purpose. Bristol was heavily bombed before the BBC could obtain possession and the tunnel became an air raid shelter. The BBC were compelled to fall back upon their second choice, the disused cliff railway tunnel, which was by no means as suitable due to the steep inclination of the trackbed. Nevertheless, within three months, four large chambers, one above the other, had been constructed within the tunnel, and three smaller chambers were provided near ground level. Within this confined space, a fully equipped transmitter, including studio and recording-rooms, was installed. The lower chambers contained an emergency generator to supply power if the mains supply failed, and a canteen with supplies of food and water sufficient for several weeks was provided. A special ventilation plant was installed, and full precautions were taken against the possibility of a gas attack. Although the transmitter was a key point in the wartime distribution of radio programmes all over the world, the extreme emergency for which it was primarily designed, never arose.

The demand for a cliff railway at Bridgnorth was first made at a public meeting called by a Mr R. Harrison in the early part of 1890. The need for some form of mechanical lift to connect the two districts of Bridgnorth known as High Town and Low Town had long been felt by the local people. The existing pedestrian access necessitated negotiating some 200 steps and long sloping footpaths. The road link between the two areas of the town was an even longer and more circuitous route.

George Marks noticed a report of the meeting in the *Birmingham Post*, the local morning newspaper, and immediately made contact with the Town Mayor. He made several subsequent visits to Bridgnorth in order to survey possible sites and a meeting was arranged with the Town Council. George Newnes' lawyer, Mr Godfrey Cooper, supported George Marks in laying before the Council several proposals supported by fully detailed plans for the construction of a water balance cliff railway, and the Council were clearly impressed. Upon completion of all the negotiations a new limited liability company styled The Bridgnorth Castle Hill Railway Company was registered in the early part of 1891. George Newnes, who once again had agreed to provide the initial finance, was appointed Chairman. J. Whitefoot was appointed Deputy Chairman, to safeguard the Town's interests, and George Croydon Marks, Director and Engineer. Other Directors were R. Margetts, J. W. McMichael and J. Pratt. Godfrey Cooper was Company Secretary. Work on the construction of the railway commenced on 7 March 1891.

The track was cut out of red sandstone rock and the sleepers were secured by bolts to large concrete blocks let into the rock bed at intervals. The length of the track was 200 ft having a vertical rise of 118 ft, and, as at Lynton and Clifton, the 3 ft 8 in. gauge was selected. The two tracks were parallel throughout their length, and due to the limited space available at the top of the incline, the rope pulleys were mounted almost horizontally, necessitating leading-off pulleys at the top end of the track to direct the ropes from the inclined to the horizontal position. The water for filling the upper car tanks was drawn from a reservoir in the High Town and discharged into another reservoir under the engine room in the Low Town. Duplicated Baker 'Forward' gas engines and pumps were employed for pumping water up to the High Town reservoir, so that the same water was used over and over again. The braking systems and other mechanical features were all exactly as employed on the Clifton Railway.

The line was opened on 7 July 1892 at a ceremony performed by the Mayor of Bridgnorth and the occasion was marked by a local public holiday. Unlike the other cliff railways, which operated on a seasonal basis, the Castle Hill Railway operated throughout the year, closing only on Christmas Day, performing a valuable, uninterrupted public service for forty years. In April 1933, a locally unpopular decision was taken to close the line, but after much local agitation the company was acquired by new owners, who promptly re-opened the line in May 1934. The water balance system of operation was abandoned in 1944, and replaced by electrically operated constant haulage gear supplied by Metropolitan Vickers, which enabled the two car conductors to be dispensed with. In 1955 smart new car bodies were built by a local Stourbridge firm, and happily, the railway continues to operate daily, and looks like reaching its centenary.

Any scheme of benefit to the people of Matlock in Derbyshire, was of special interest to George Newnes for it was at Matlock Bath, in the old Manse, Glenorchy House, that he was born in March 1851. He was the youngest of six children of the Congregational minister, the Rev. Thomas Mold Newnes and his Scottish wife, Sarah. At the age of ten George was despatched to Silcoates Hall, near Wakefield, a boarding school for Congregational ministers' sons. He then went on to Shireland Hall School, near Birmingham. Following a period at the City of London School, he was apprenticed to a wholesaler in the fancy goods trade, but always retained his great affection for Matlock. Glenorchy House was a large, dignified, eighteenth-century country house, with gardens bordering the River Derwent. It was an ideal place for a growing family. In later life George Newnes often recalled how as a young apprentice living in London, he thirsted for the peace and tranquillity of his old home.

The credit for the original idea of building a street tramway in Matlock belongs to Bob Smith, a local man, who in 1862 spent some time in San Francisco. He was greatly impressed with the city's new cable trams, which were the first of their kind in the world. Over a period of twenty-five years he unsuccessfully tried to gain support for a similar system in Matlock. Neither John Smedley, the wealthy local hosiery manufacturer and principal employer in the town, nor the Matlock Local Board would listen to him. Hearing about the successful opening of the Lynton & Lynmouth Cliff Railway, Smith, who was now an elected member of the Local Board, decided to re-open the matter and called a public meeting. By coincidence, George Marks read a report of this meeting in the *High Peak News* and immediately advised his friend George Newnes of the situation. Newnes wrote to Smith on 20 June 1890, claiming, 'I am in a better position than anyone else, in consequence of certain valuable patents, to carry out a scheme such as you envisage.' By the same post he sent George Marks a cheque for £1000 with instructions to carry out a survey and submit a detailed report, adding that he would be willing to provide the necessary finance for the project.

The technical report and detailed plans submitted by George Marks, and the financial proposals put forward by George Newnes were accepted by the local authority. In 1891 they agreed to the formation of the Matlock Tramway Company having a nominal capital of £20,000. George Newnes was appointed Chairman; Bob Smith, Managing Director; George Marks, Engineer; together with four other members of the Local Board; and Miles Sleigh was appointed Secretary. After lengthy consultation, Dick, Kerr & Company, well known in the field of urban tramway construction, were given the contract for building the line at a figure of £10,000. The contract for building the engine house, tram depot, workshops and company offices to plans prepared by Mr John Turner, a local architect, was awarded to W. Knowles & Son at £2600.

The problems associated with the design of the half-mile-long, steep incline tramway, with its numerous curves and gradients varying from 1 in 5.5 to 1 in 15, were unique and very different from those encountered in a short, straight, constant gradient cliff railway. Wisely, George Marks persuaded his colleagues to appoint the well-known tramway engineer, Mr W. N. Colam, as Consultant Engineer to the Company. Colam had already acquired considerable experience as Engineer to cable tramways in London, Birmingham and Edinburgh. George also brought in his brother Edward as Resident Engineer, responsible for the day-to-day supervision of the construction work. George's commitments in London and Birmingham and at the Clifton Rocks and Bridgnorth cliff railway sites made it impossible for him to devote more than two or three days a month to the Matlock scheme. Construction work commenced in March 1892 and fortunately James More, a competent young site engineer employed by Dick, Kerr & Company, worked well with Edward Marks. Later, More was named as joint patentee with George Marks in Patent No. 19,200 filed in October 1892, describing improved methods of braking tramcars.

The 3 ft 6 in. gauge tramway operated from Crown Square, near Matlock Bridge, climbing Bank Road and Smedley Street, to the new engine house and depot built in Rutland Street, a rise of 300 ft in a distance of 2500 ft. The single track system had a passing loop in Smedley Street. Two horizontal steam engines installed in the

The Matlock steep incline tramway.

engine house drove a continuously moving steel haulage cable through friction clutches, at a constant speed of 6 m.p.h. The cable was located in a box section channel built into the roadway under the tramway. A clasp arrangement mounted underneath the tram-car bogies passed through the slot in the roadway into the cable box, and gripped the moving cable in the manner of a closed hand. The driver controlled the operation of gripping and releasing the moving cable when starting and stopping. Additionally, he had at his disposal a hand-operated screw brake working on the bogie wheel rims, and a foot-operated gripper brake working on the underside of the central slot in the cable box.

The three spendidly appointed double-decker tramcars purchased by the Company were built by Milnes & Company of Birkenhead. Each accommodated thirty-one seated passengers, and the seat backs were reversible, so that the passengers always faced the direction of travel. The vehicles each weighed 4.5 tons, including the gripper gear, and they were painted and lined out to the highest standards of the day.

The gradient in Bank Road made the line the steepest in the world to traverse a public roadway. So unusual was the system that General Hutchinson, RE, HM Chief Inspector of Railways' personally supervised the final acceptance trials. Until the Board of

Trade's Certificate of Approval was received, the line could not be opened to the public. Fortunately, all went according to plan, and the grand opening ceremony took place on 28 March 1893.

George Newnes's wife, Priscilla, officially opened the tramway at a lavishly prepared ceremony in the presence of local civic dignitaries, who were accompanied by the local Yeomanry, in full dress uniform. The opening was followed by a splendid public Banquet in the Assembly Rooms, where everybody seemed to be on their feet making speeches of praise. It is doubtful if Matlock has seen anything like it, before or since. It was certainly a memorable day for both George and Edward Marks. The story of these events is told in detail in a delightful little book published by the Arkwright Society in 1972. Sadly, the tramway was never a financial success. During the first twenty years' operations to 1913, it made modest losses amounting to £800, but after World War I these increased to £1000 a year, and in September 1927, the Local Authority, by a substantial majority, took the decision to close the line.

Municipality-owned electric lighting was very much in vogue by 1890. Many Local Authorities throughout the country were busily engaged acquiring their own electric generators and distribution facilities. A natural outcome of this demand was the emergence of specialist contracting firms able to install and in some cases operate the new machinery. Bourne & Grant of London were such a company. In the early 1890s they secured a contract for the installation of steam-powered generators built by John Fowler & Co. of Leeds, and street lighting in the Mid-Wales coastal town of Aberystwyth. Some of this plant actually survived in working order until the 1970s. Thomas Grant, one of the partners in the firm, liked the area and took up residence in the town, launching an ambitious scheme for the development of Aberystwyth as a tourist attraction. He purchased the pier, and undertook urgently needed restoration work; he opened a new steam laundry in King Street; and laid plans for a cliff railway to the summit of Constitution Hill, a 500-ft-high hill at the northern end of the promenade. Although Grant had originally qualified as a Civil Engineer, he soon became a specialist in electrical installation work. He patented an improved dynamo and a new electric lamp before he was twenty-five. Unfortunately, at the age of thirty-three, with a very promising career ahead, he contracted typhoid fever and died.

Layout for Constitutional Hill, Aberystwyth.

His partner, John Bourne, and his widow decided to continue
Grant's work in Aberystwyth. After several months' negotiations to
secure the financial position, they were introduced to George
Marks, who was very enthusiastic about their plans. In June 1895,
the Aberystwyth Improvement Company was formed, with George
Marks as Managing Director and John Bourne and Jessie Grant as
Directors. Restoration of the pier was completed, and a rather
splendid Pavilion, which George Marks personally designed, was
added to the entrance. It was agreed that the old Hotel Cambria
near the railway station should be modernized, and new boilers and
other modern plant were ordered for the King Street laundry. It
was also decided that the Constitutional Hill cliff railway should
operate on Marks's water balance principle, and that the surrounding area should be laid out with ornamental gardens, with shelters,
kiosks and a fairground switchback ride. George Marks agreed that
he would make the 6½-hour train journey from London to
Aberystwyth every two weeks to supervise the work during the
construction period.

Work was started on the railway in October 1895, and £60,000
was set aside for excavation work, which involved removing some
12,000 tons of faulty shale and other debris from an old quarry. The
main excavation was 400 ft long and the overall length of the line

Aberystwyth cliff railway 'toast-rack' passenger car.

was 800 ft at a ruling gradient of 1 in 2. The upper portion of the line was slightly steeper than the remainder, and the gradient at the half-way point was eased to allow the two 4 ft 10 in. gauge tracks to diverge in order to provide adequate clearance for the cars as they passed one another. The main excavation was traversed by four bridges carrying footpaths across the line, and concrete retaining walls lined the cutting. Concrete also provided the trackbed for the wooden sleepers and flat-bottom steel rails. Worthington compound steam engines and pumps were installed for pumping the water required for operating the water balance system from a reservoir adjacent to the lower station, to another at the summit.

Marks abandoned the flat-floor-type passenger car, mounted on a

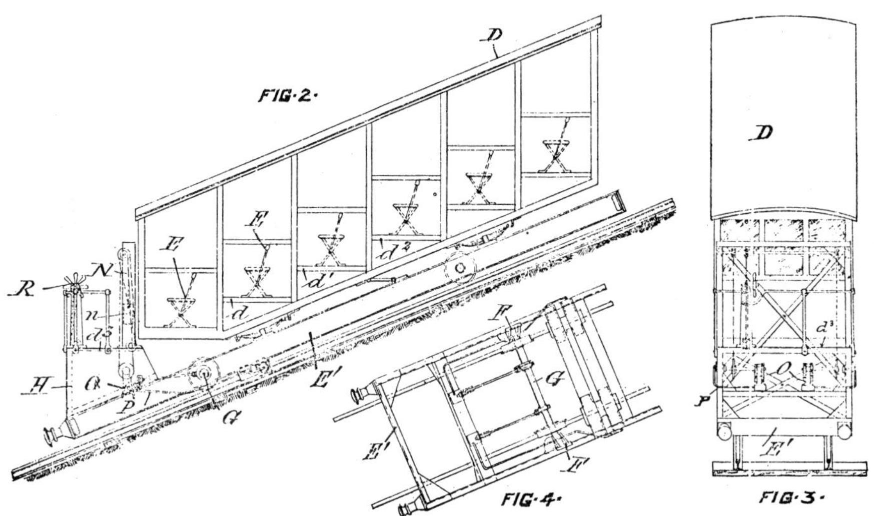

Drawing attached to patent specification No. 10,457 of 1895 depicting the Aberystwyth cliff railway car.

triangular frame as used at Lynton, Clifton and Bridgnorth, in favour of a stepped-floor 'toast-rack'-type car arranged to carry thirty passengers seated across the width of the car. The backs of the seats were reversible, enabling the passengers to face the same direction as the car was travelling. The unmanned upper and lower station platforms were stepped to corrrespond with the steps in the passenger cars. These features were all described in Marks's Provisional Patent No. 10,457 filed in 1895. The method of operation, the four independent braking systems, and other mechanical details were exactly as described in his earlier Patent No. 9535 of 1888.

It was planned that the rebuilt pier, its smart new pavilion, and the cliff railway should be officially opened on 26 June 1896, during a visit of the then Prince and Princess of Wales. The Prince's three-feather motif was incorporated in the brickwork of the lower station entrance, and was boldly displayed on the front panels of the two passenger cars. Unfortunately, in May, George Marks's health suffered another set-back, and the final acceptance trials on the railway had to be delayed. The opening finally took place in a festive atmosphere on Saturday, 1 August, to the accompaniment of the Newtown Silver Band.

Marks soon became a well-known figure in Aberystwyth and he made many friends, including the distinguished engineer Sir James

View of Constitutional Hill from Aberstwyth Pier, c. 1898.

Szlumper, who was inextricably involved with the tragi-comic proposals for a main-line railway from Manchester to Milford Haven in Pembrokeshire, traversing the Principality from north to south. The first scheme launched in 1860 was abandoned when the line's northerly progress was diverted to Aberystwyth at Strata Florida, avoiding the Vale of Rheidol. The scheme lay dormant until Aberystwyth became popular with tourists in the 1890s, and during the construction of the Cliff Railway, George Marks assisted

Szlumper to survey a new line. This ran due east from Aberystwyth, along the Vale of Rheidol and beyond to connect eventually with the London & North Western Railway. The prime objective of the scheme was to bring Aberystwyth within two hours' travelling time of Birmingham and four hours from London. A Bill, known as the East & West Wales Railway Bill, was placed before Parliament, reaching the Committee stage, but was then thrown out due to the inadequacy of the arrangements for financing the estimated £700,000 initial cost. Had this project succeeded, it seems probable that the longer-term prosperity of Aberystwyth would have been assured.

Eventually, due mainly to pressure from the local iron foundries and the owners of the iron ore and sulphur mines in the Vale of Rheidol, the Light Railway Commissioners authorized the building of a narrow gauge railway. It was 12 miles long and ran from Aberystwyth harbour to Devil's Bridge, rising to a height of 680 ft above sea level. This delightful 1 ft 11 5/8 in. gauge railway continues to operate today as the only remaining steam-hauled railway wholly owned by British Railways.

So completely did George Marks become identified with Aberystwyth that in 1897 he successfully stood for election to the Town Council. He concentrated his election campaign upon issues of special interest to the local people: (1) A call for further improvements in tourist facilities; (2) Improved railway connections with the West Midlands, thereby greatly reducing the travelling time to London, and (3) Improvements to local workers' housing. The following year he was appointed a Justice of the Peace and sat on the Aberystwyth Bench. In 1898 the Aberystwyth Improvement Company acquired additional capital from a Suffolk gentleman, Sir Thomas Tacon, and further investments were made in new swimming baths, a hotel, shops and a theatre. The development of Constitutional Hill was completed, which included a refreshment room, a reading-room, a large greenhouse containing many rare and exotic plants, and a rather splendid, ornate ballroom was built in the old quarry behind the top station. Marks also became associated with improvements to the harbour and the building of a new Customs House, which became necessary as more and more ore from the local mines and the finished products of George Green's ironfoundry were exported. Later this foundry produced many of the castings and fabrications used in the construction of the

Sir George Newnes.

famous Sydney Harbour Bridge, which were shipped direct to Australia.

In 1903 Sir Thomas Tacon took over control of the Aberystwyth Improvement Company, which does not seem to have been a great financial success. Ten years later, Tacon sold his interests to another Suffolk gentleman, Mr Charles Liebbrand of Felixstowe, and George Marks's connections with Aberystwyth appear to have ended about this time.

The cliff railway continued to operate under various owners and in the 1920s the water balance system was replaced by 55 h.p. Morley electric motors installed at the top station. The power supply was taken from the town's generators and converted to 440 volts d.c. by a mercury-arc rectifier and transformer housed in the old engine house at the lower station. The system remained virtually unaltered until 1976, when the present owners, the Aberystwyth Cliff Railway Company, acquired the railway. They carried out extensive repairs and modifications to the cars, track and platforms, and installed a sophisticated, labour-saving automatic control system and safety gear. A novel feature of the electrical system is that when the cars are travelling under their own momentum, the electric haulage motors automatically become electric generators and actually supply electricity to the National Grid, greatly reducing the railway's operating costs. Today, the Cliff Railway is a member of the Great Little Trains of Wales organization, and hopefully will continue to operate for many years to come, as an interesting example of our engineering heritage.

The last of Marks's nineteenth-century water-balance-operated cliff railways was built in Hungary. In 1894 he had received the honour of being appointed Consulting Engineer to the Duke of Saxe-Coburg Gotha, the brother of Prince Albert, the late Prince Consort. In 1896 he was authorized to build a cliff railway in Budapest. Regrettably few precise details of the line have survived two World Wars. All that is known is that it ascends from the banks of the River Danube to the historic Blocksberg fortress on the outskirts of the city and is still operating. An early photograph indicates a line similar to the Constitutional Hill Railway, with stepped 'toast-rack'-type cars, and the line terminating inside the fortress. So pleased were the Hungarians with their new cliff railway, they invited George Marks and his wife to join the Royal Party in September 1896, at the grand opening ceremony to mark the inauguration of the new iron gates on the Lower Danube. Later, the Duke of Saxe-Coburg Gotha conferred upon Marks the Cross of a Knight of the Ducal Order of Ernest. Undoubtedly George Marks greatly enjoyed his visits to the Austro-Hungarian empire at its zenith and was greatly flattered by the award.

An interesting aside to this appointment demonstrates the prejudices current in nineteenth-century Europe. In 1896 George Marks was advised to issue a statement to the Press Association, stating that he was not connected with the Jewish faith, either by

The Budapest cliff railway rising from the banks of the River Danube.

birth or education. About the same time he dropped the name style Mr George Marks, and let it be known that in future he wished to be referred to as Mr G. Croydon Marks. No doubt, he felt that this sounded more dignified and stylish when addressing a successful Consulting Engineer and Patent Agent.

Chapter 5
The Partnership (1894–1913)

Six years after establishing his business in Birmingham, George Croydon Marks decided that it was both necessary and opportune to formalize his relationship with his Partners, Dugald Clerk and his brother, Edward Marks. An agreement between the three men was signed and sealed on 1 January 1894. The Partnership Capital, initially fixed at £2000, was held entirely by Croydon Marks and Dugald Clerk. Edward was admitted for a trial period of two years, without contributing any working capital. It was agreed that in the first year, each Partner should receive a salary of £125, and that the profits should be allocated on the basis of five-twelfths to Croydon Marks, five-twelfths to Dugald Clerk and two-twelfths to Edward Marks. In the second year, this was altered, four-tenths of the profits going to each of the Senior Partners and two-tenths to Edward Marks. Upon completion of two years' service, Edward Marks was given an equal share of the profits, and admitted into full partnership. The Partnership capital was simultaneously increased to £2800.

In the same year, the three Partners became Fellows of the Chartered Institute of Patent Agents. The Institute had been Incorporated by Royal Charter in 1891, and their election to the highest grade of membership confirmed their professional status as Patent Agents. George Croydon Marks's, and to a lesser extent Edward Marks's, involvement with Cliff Railways and Steep Incline Tramways, had been both challenging and enjoyable, and earned them a measure of public recognition they would not otherwise have received. However, it seems doubtful whether any of the schemes had proved particularly lucrative. During the next twenty-five years the three men concentrated on the development of their Partnership into a successful and highly respected International Patent Agency. When George Croydon Marks received his knighthood in 1911, a leading national newspaper commented, 'Sir George founded Marks & Clerk, and his firm is now recognised as the greatest firm of its kind in the world', comment which no doubt gave the Partners enormous satisfaction.

During 1894 Croydon Marks received his first commission from the United States. Acting on behalf of The Hogan Engineering Company of New York, he filed British Patent No. 2016, describing several unique features of a large land-type water tube boiler. The first successful design of this type of boiler was patented by G. H. Babcock and S. Wilcox in the United States in 1867. It soon became popular worldwide, as the steam generator most suitable for use with the Hon. Charles Parsons's steam turbines and electricity generators. It provided a large heating surface for steam raising, was inherently safer than the conventional shell-type boiler, and the weight of water in the boiler was smaller, so that steam could be raised more quickly.

This commission was the first of many Marks & Clerk subsequently received from North American companies, and provided the foundation for a long and profitable association with the United States. In the next thirty-five years Croydon Marks crossed the North Atlantic more than thirty times. He always greatly enjoyed the comfort and luxury of the great trans-Atlantic liners. He made many friends and valuable business contacts during these crossings. It is sad that present-day businessmen have neither the time, nor the opportunity, of enjoying this memorable experience.

At home the new Partnership continued to handle many notable Patent registrations connected with the development of the motor-car and motor-cycle. Mention has already been made of the pioneers, Lanchester and Lucas. Soon instructions followed from the other leaders in the industry, including W. & E. Allday of Allday & Onions; Herbert Austin, later Lord Austin; Lord Nuffield's Morris engine factory in Coventry; and the motor-cycle manufacturers Rudge Whitworth and Velocette. Most of this work was transacted by Edward Marks at the Birmingham office. He also handled work for other prominent Midlands firms such as the steel tube manufacturers Stewart & Lloyds and Reynolds Tubes; the railway vehicle manufacturers Metropolitan Carriage & Wagon Company; Heenan & Froude, makers of dynamometers and other engine testing equipment; Warne Wright & Rowland, high-volume turned part manufacturers; and Rippingille's of Aston, pioneer manufacturers of paraffin-oil-fired domestic appliances.

Edward Marks became a recognized authority on the subjects of the strength of materials and the manufacture of iron and steel

Sir Dugald Clerk in academic robes.

tubes, and many leading companies frequently sought his professional advice. In 1897 he wrote a definitive book entitled, *The Manufacture of Iron and Steel Tubes*, which went to a second edition in 1903. In the following year he published another book entitled, *Modern Small Arms and Ammunition*, based on the experience and knowledge he had acquired handling Kynoch's patent work. Both these books were published by Marks & Clerk, who for many years retained an interest in publishing. Edward Marks also became a visiting lecturer at the Birmingham Central Technical College, and from 1895 to 1898 was President of the College Engineering Society. He greatly admired the younger generation, and never missed an opportunity of helping any student who showed interest and promise in his work.

Croydon Marks took his first articled pupil, William Evans, shortly before leaving Birmingham. In due course Evans joined him in London, and passed his qualifying examinations in 1897. Three years later he left Marks & Clerk to set up on his own account, taking with him the valuable Anglo-Iranian Oil Company account. The second pupil to qualify in 1900 was Matthew Atkinson Adam. Following his graduation as an engineer, he spent some time working with Lord Kelvin, the famous physicist, before joining Marks & Clerk as an articled pupil. Adam was the first outsider to be admitted to the Marks & Clerk Partnership, and for many years worked closely with Dugald Clerk, acting as an Expert Witness in many important Patent Law cases. During the first twenty years of the Partnership to 1913, seventeen articled clerks successfully passed their qualifying examinations under Croydon Marks's careful tuition and supervision and many later reached the top of their profession.

Throughout this period Dugald Clerk's reputation continued to grow. He was widely accepted in industry, in the academic world, and by the legal profession, as a man of great wisdom and understanding. He served as a Council Member of the Chartered Institute of Patent Agents from 1904 to 1914. The Junior Institution of Engineers elected him as its President in 1905, and two years later he became President of the Society of British Gas Industries. This body successfully brought together the supply, distribution, plant and appliance sections of the gas engineering profession. In 1908 Dugald Clerk became a full member of both the Institution of Civil Engineers, and the Institution of Mechanical Engineers. Shortly before his death in 1932 he was elected President of the 'Civils', but sadly ill-health prevented him taking office. He served on the Council of the Institution of Mechanical Engineers from 1911 to 1917, and was a Vice-President from 1917 to 1919. Undoubtedly, the honour which pleased him most was his election as a Fellow of the Royal Society in 1908. Founded under the patronage of Charles II, and his scientifically minded cousin, Prince Rupert, this august body has always strived to promote the idea of law in the Universe, and encouraged scientific methods of enquiry to discover truth. It has long maintained that these methods would never lead to conclusions inconsistent with Biblical

Matthew Atkinson Adam, the first outside Partner and close collaborator of Sir Dugald Clerk.

history and miraculous religion. The overwhelming majority of its distinguished members have, for three centuries, lived and died in that faith.

Clerk's definitive work on the gas and oil engine, published originally in 1886, was revised in 1896, and again in 1909, when it was split into two volumes. When one recalls the extraordinarily rapid developments in internal combustion engine technology in the intervening years, it is amazing that this work justified re-issuing twenty-three years after it made its first appearance.

In the period under review, Clerk presented the following major papers, before various learned bodies:

    1905 – Coal Gas and its Rivals for Motive Power
    1907 – Flame in Gas and Petrol Motors
    1907 – Limits of Thermal Efficiency in I/C Motors
    1907 – Science and Practice
    1907 – Present Position of Gas and Petrol Engines
    1913 – The Working Fluid of I/C Engines

In addition to his seat on Kynoch's Board, Dugald Clerk was invited to join the Board of the National Gas Engine Company of Ashton-under-Lyne in 1908. The Company was founded in 1889, and initially concentrated upon the manufacture of horizontal-type gas engines. Shortly after Dugald Clerk's appointment the works were substantially enlarged to include the production of vertical-type engines. A few years later diesel engines were introduced and after the Great War production was turned over entirely to this type of engine, in sizes ranging from 3.5 b.h.p. to 1840 b.h.p. The Company built up an enviable reputation for quality and reliability and specialized in the manufacture of engines for industrial and marine applications. In 1929 Dugald Clerk became the Company's Chairman, but ill-health forced his retirement in 1932.

Matthew Atkinson Adam, the second Articled Clerk to pass his qualifying examinations under Croydon Marks's tuition, was admitted into the Partnership under the terms of a new agreement drawn up in 1901. His remuneration was originally fixed at £300 a year, plus a one-tenth share of the profits. Under the terms of this agreement, the original Partners each drew £1000 a year and shared equally nine-tenths of the profits, which that year amounted to £3126. In 1905 Clerk and Adam established an Engineering Laboratory at 6 Featherstone Buildings, and thereafter operated independently of the Patent Agency as Consulting Engineers. Dugald Clerk retired in 1931 and Adam carried on the laboratory until his own death in 1939. The principal work they undertook upon behalf of Marks & Clerk was as expert witnesses in Patent Law litigation, an area in which both excelled.

An expert witness is examined on oath, but at the same time his position is generally recognized as in some respects that of an advocate for the side which retains his services. There are limits in advocacy beyond which an honourable man, whether on oath or not, will refuse to go. A large measure of Dugald Clerk's success was his proper appreciation of this fact. He was an admirable witness and a most persuasive advocate. He espoused with warmth any cause which he advocated, and naturally identified himself with the client. He was keenly alive to the damage done to a cause by slovenly presentation, whether by Counsel or witness, and always prepared his case with minute care and attention to detail.

In 1906 Dugald Clerk spent three months in the United States as an expert witness in the famous Selden *versus* Ford Motor Company suit. It was one of the longest legal battles in American history, and dragged on for six years. The case was brought by a group of car manufacturers who tried to stifle growing competition from the remarkable Henry Ford. They based their case upon a somewhat vague patent filed in 1879 by George B. Selden, an American Patent Attorney. Selden took little part in the case and died during the hearing. The background to the case and its outcome is best told in Henry Ford's own words.

'We were harried by a big suit brought against the company to try to force us into line with an association of automobile manufacturers, who were operating under the false principle that there was only a limited market for automobiles and that a monopoly of that market was essential. This was the famous Selden Patent suit, the defense of which at times, severely strained our resources. It was the association which sought the monopoly, and the situation was this.

'Selden filed an application as far back as 1879 for a patent the object of which was stated to be, "The production of a safe, simple and cheap road locomotive, light in weight, easy to control, possessed of sufficient power to overcome an ordinary inclination." This application was kept alive in the Patent Office, by methods which are perfectly legal, until 1895, when the patent was granted. In 1879, when the application was filed, the automobile was practically unknown to the general public, but by the time the patent was issued everybody was familiar with self-propelled vehicles, and most men, including myself, who had been for years working on motor propulsion, were surprised to learn that what we had made practicable was covered by an application years before, although the applicant had kept his idea merely as an idea. He had done nothing to put it into practice.

'The specific claims under the patent were divided into six groups and I think, that not a single one of them was a really new idea even in 1879. The Patent Office allowed a combination and issued a so-called "Combination Patent", deciding that the combination (A) of a carriage with its body machinery and steering wheel, with the (B) propelling mechanism, clutch and gear, and finally, (C) the engine, made a valid patent.

'With all of that we are not concerned. I believed that my engine had nothing whatsoever in common with what Selden had in mind. The powerful combination of manufacturers who called themselves the "Licensed Manufacturers", because they operated under licenses from the patentee, brought suit against us as we began to be a factor in motor production. We took volumes of testimony, and the blow came on September 15th, 1909, when Judge Hough rendered an opinion in the District Court finding against us. Immediately the Licensed Association began to advertise, warning prospective purchasers against our cars. They had done the same thing in 1903 at the start of the suit when it was thought that we could be put out of business. It was a considerable blow to get the first decision against us, for we believed that many buyers would be frightened away by threats of court action against individual buyers. The idea was spread that if the suit finally went against me, every man who owned a Ford car would be prosecuted. It was said that a man buying a Ford car might as well be buying a ticket to jail. We answered with four page advertisements in the principal newspapers all over the country, offering every owner of a Ford car the protection of a $12 million bond.'

'We thought that the bond would give assurance to the buyers, but less than fifty people asked for them. Probably nothing so well advertised the Ford car and the Ford Motor Company as did this suit, and that year we sold more than 18,000 cars. Prosecuting that suit was probably one of the most shortsighted acts that any group of American businessmen has ever combined to commit. I regard it as most fortunate for the country's automobile manufacturers that we eventually won, and the Licensed Association ceased to be a serious factor in the business.'

Upon another occasion when speaking about competition, Ford commented,

'Competition is supposed to be a menace, and all too frequently management circumvents its competitors, establishing monopolies by artificial means. They seem to have the same idea that so many trade unions have – the ridiculous notion that more profit can be had doing less work than more.'

In the intervening years since Ford uttered these words, both American management and unions appear to have learned these lessons, but perhaps in the United Kingdom we still have some way to go.

Politically always a Liberal at heart, Croydon Marks was not averse to criticizing British management attitudes and in 1907, when industry was still dominated by small and medium-sized family businesses, he publicly made the following comments:

'Some British manufacturers have a peculiar habit of keeping the nature of their business a secret in the district where they reside and within the social circle they cultivate. With the object of masking their actual pursuits they effect an interest in Stocks and Shares, or in rural and country pursuits, sports and pastimes. Where this spirit prevails and where neither pride or pleasure is developed in the business, it is not surprising that suggestions for improvement are not appreciated and that opportunities for betterment of output are ignored. The sons and successors of those who founded business undertakings frequently ignore such industries and evince neither desire, nor aptitude for keeping to the front or leading with new features in the commercial race. Habits of indolence lead to the rejection of proposals that would involve any alterations to plant, the scrapping of old machines, and the adoption of more modern methods for economically meeting the demands of new markets. Consequently foreign competitors are constantly encouraged to embark against them.'

Whilst Croydon Marks was busily engaged in London developing the firm as an International Patent Agency, concentrating particularly upon his American connections, Edward was quietly extending the work of the Birmingham and Manchester offices. The decision to open a branch in Manchester had been fully justified by the result obtained during its first ten years' operations. In 1901, the established Manchester practice of P. J. Livsey was acquired, bringing several important new clients to the Partnership, and by 1910, it was found necessary to remove to larger offices at 25 Market Street. In Birmingham, the practice of C. J. Powell was purchased and Herbert Kerslake, formerly editor of *Practical Engineering*, who had passed his qualifying examinations in 1904, was sent to manage the firm. Later, in 1913, when Kerslake was sent to the United States, C. J. Powell was merged with Marks & Clerk's Birmingham office. The number of Patent applications made by the Birmingham and Manchester offices increased year by year under Edward Marks's stewardship, and the Partnership annual profits continued to show a satisfactory growth. In the twenty years 1894 to 1913, the Partnership capital increased from £2000 to £40,000.

Edward's business life was helped by the contented family life he and Lily enjoyed together with their three children, living in Edgbaston. The eldest child, Gladys Ella, was born in 1897. She was educated at Cheltenham Ladies' College and married Percy Russell, a son of Edward's old friends in Leicester. Two years later,

Edward Marks's family, including his wife Lily, his three children, and his sisters Amelia and Emily.

in 1899, a son, Arthur Houlton Marks, was born. He was educated at Mill Hill School in North London, and read for his Bachelor of Arts degree at Lincoln College, Oxford. Later he qualified as a solicitor and joined Coote & Co., who were Marks & Clerk's lawyers and whose offices were also in Lincoln's Inn Fields. In 1922 he published a fascinating little book entitled, *Historical Notes on Lincoln's Inn Fields*, tracing the history of this pleasant London square back to the Middle Ages. Arthur Marks married Clara Scuddards of Ilkley, and they had three children. Sadly, he died during World War II, at the early age of forty-five. Edward and Lily's third child, Ralph Croydon Marks, was born in 1903. He spent his adult life in the motor trade in Birmingham and London. He died in 1967, leaving a widow and two sons, his third son having died some years earlier in his twenties.

Mrs Russell, Aunt Ella to her nieces and nephews, described the Marks family as, 'Always united in spirit, but divided geographically.' William and Amelia continued to live quietly in Eltham, with their two daughters, Amelia and Emily, after William's retirement from the Royal Arsenal in 1898. Once Marks & Clerk became established in London, both sisters were employed by the firm. Emily resigned in 1906 upon her marriage to Charles Chapman of Cardiff. Amelia, who never married, continued to work in the accounts office at Lincoln's Inn Fields until she retired in the mid-1930s. The rest of the family used to visit William and Amelia upon every possible occasion, although they were all in the habit of spending Christmas with George and Maggie, wherever they were living at the time. In later life George Marks once commented that he and his wife had lived in sixteen homes since their marriage. Maggie Marks always did her utmost to preserve the family unit and to ensure their comfort and pleasure whenever they were in her home. Both within and outside the immediate family circle she was acknowledged as a kind and considerate hostess. No doubt, her constant concern for her family, both on her own side, as well as her husband's, in some measure resulted from the great sadness in her married life, for she was unable to have children of her own.

In 1911 Edward Marks was persuaded to stand as a Liberal candidate for the Rotten Park Ward of Birmingham City Council, which he won comfortably. He rendered the City valuable service for many years, and although staunchly Liberal in his attitudes, he maintained that voting in the Council Chamber should not be on party lines. He became a member of the Electricity Supply Committee, which at the time was unpopular with the citizens of Birmingham, due to the unsatisfactory performance of the Tramways Department. Eventually, they became widely acknowledged as one of the most efficient municipal transport services in the country. Edward always campaigned for cheap electricity, rather than using the profits of the Electricity Supply Department to reduce the rates. Central Government might well take note of this philosophy today, as British industry struggles to compete with the lower wages and lower energy costs enjoyed by many of our overseas competitors. Later, Edward served with distinction on both the Town Planning and Insurance Committees. Throughout his life, Edward, like his brother, devoted a great deal of his leisure time to serving the Congregational Church. He was both Deacon and Treasurer of the Francis Road Church in Edgbaston, and later became Chairman of the Warwickshire Congregational Union.

Reverting to the business, a third Partnership Deed was signed in February 1906. This assessed the value of Goodwill as being equivalent to the combined profits earned in the two years, 1904 and 1905. The Partnership Capital was allocated in the proportions of three-eighths each to George Croydon Marks and Dugald Clerk

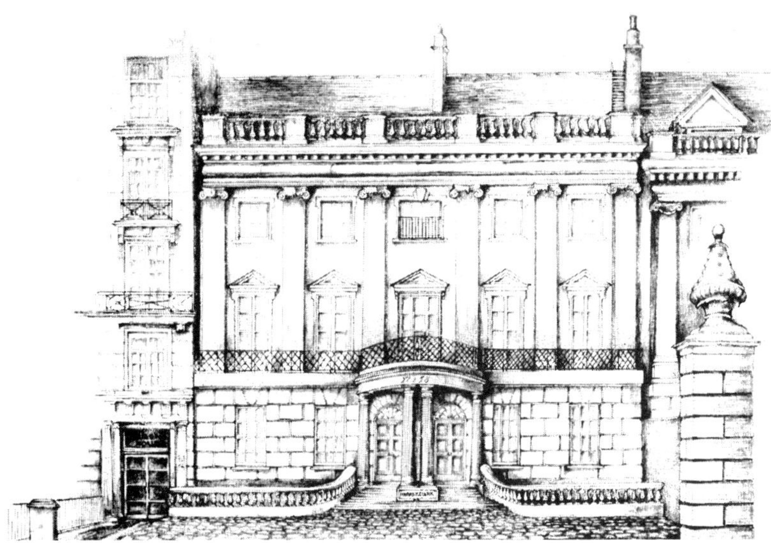

57/58 Lincoln's Inn Fields.

and two-eighths to Edward Marks, thereby formally acknowledging Edward's contribution to the success of the business. Annual profits under £4000 were split equally between the four Partners and profits over £4000 were allocated on the basis of three-tenths each to George Croydon Marks and Dugald Clerk, and two-tenths each to Edward Marks and Matthew Atkinson Adam. The validity of this agreement was extended to 31 December 1912.

While walking in Lincoln's Inn Fields one lunchtime in 1908, Atkinson Adam noticed that the lease of one of the great houses, Nos. 57/58, on the west side of the square, was for sale. In due course, the purchase was completed, and the contractors, Higgs and Hill, were engaged to carry out extensive external restoration and internal modernization of the building. The Partners eventually moved into the building in July 1909, although they continued to retain offices in Southampton Buildings for some years.

In the Middle Ages, the main road from the North to the City converged with that from Oxford and the West at Holborn. The several manors in the vicinity today form Lincoln's Inn Fields and Gray's Inn, two of the four present-day Inns of Court. A market was held at the crossroads, otherwise the whole district comprised green fields on which cattle grazed and archery was practised. In 1640, the land now known as Lincoln's Inn Fields was purchased by Sir Edward Bellingham as a speculation, and houses were built

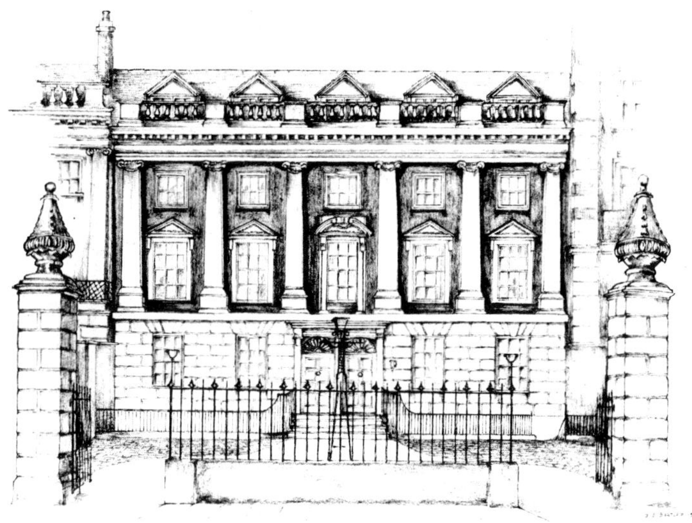

59/60 Lincoln's Inn Fields.

on three sides of the square. Nos. 57 and 58 were originally occupied as a single house. Between 1640 and the accession of Charles II there is a gap in the known history of the house. In 1666 it was acquired by the Earl of Sandwich, who was killed six years later. In 1673 ownership passed to Sir James Langham, who occupied the house until his death in 1699, and Samuel Pepys makes frequent allusion to the house in his writings. In 1708 Lord James Russell purchased the house, which then passed to Lord William Talbot, the solicitor-general in 1730, and upon his death in 1737 it was occupied by his son. Circa 1750 the second Lord Talbot completely rebuilt the house in its present grand Palladian style. In 1786 the house was acquired by the Earl of Mansfield. Later, in 1795, the property was converted into two separate houses by the distinguished architect Sir John Soane, who subsequently added the present portico and elegant staircase. When Marks & Clerk acquired the property in 1908, the two parts were again united. The partition walls were removed and complete restoration was undertaken without impairing the classic architecture.

The novelist Charles Dickens's friend, John Forster, had chambers at No. 58 from 1834 to 1856 and Dickens was a frequent visitor. In his book *Bleak House*, he described Nos. 57 and 58 Lincoln's Inn Fields as the residence of his character Mr Tulkinghorn. It was here also that Dickens read *The Chimes* to a brilliant company of friends in 1844. The Old Curiosity Shop, which Dickens immortalized, is only a stone's throw away from No. 58, on the corner of Portsmouth Street and Lincoln's Inn Fields. The half-timbered house is said to date from 1550, and to be one of the oldest houses in London.

In March 1918 Croydon Marks acquired a lease on the adjoining houses Nos. 59 and 60, for his own use. These were built in 1641 by Sir David Cunningham. They were built as a single residence and became known as 'Lindsey House', although they had no connection with that family. In 1751 the house was divided into two town houses by Isaac Ware, an architect of the Inigo Jones school, and the classical style of Inigo Jones is still indelibly stamped on the house. Like its neighbour, the divided house was occupied by several distinguished people, including the Hon. Spencer Perceval, the Prime Minister, who was assassinated in the lobby of the House of Commons in 1812. Croydon Marks reunited the two houses into one, and had a flat made for his own use. He established his publishing business, the Hertford Record Company, on the ground floor. In 1913 the Partnership rented Lindsey House from Croydon Marks, and upon his death in 1938 his will included a provision giving his Partners the option of purchasing the 99-year lease for the sum of £20,000.

In June 1911, on the occasion of King George V's Coronation, George Croydon Marks received the honour of a knighthood for public and political Services. He received a letter from 10 Downing Street, signed personally by Mr Asquith, the Prime Minister, informing him of the King's command, but this story belongs to another chapter. Henceforth, only thirty-five years after starting his career as an impecunious apprentice at Woolwich Arsenal, he became Sir George Croydon Marks. At the time of his Knighthood Sir George and Lady Marks were living in a pleasant house, 'St Bernards', at Caterham in Surrey, having removed from London two or three years earlier. In 1909 he had been appointed a Justice of the Peace for the County of Surrey and sat on the Caterham Bench.

In 1911 the Partnership capital stood at £34,000, and the number of Patent registrations handled by the firm continued to grow each year. Applications filed in the four years prior to the outbreak of World War I, a period when industry on both sides of the Atlantic was booming, clearly illustrates the firm's success and the importance of its overseas connections.

Charles Dickens reading to a group of friends at 57/58 Lincoln's Inn Fields.

Sir George Marks's activities in the United States in the period 1895 to 1910 proved so successful that in November 1910 the Partners decided to establish a branch office in New York. His friend Thomas Alva Edison, whom he first met in 1890, and became one of Marks & Clerk's most important clients, once said of him, 'George Marks is as well known in the United States as he is in his own country.' Offices were leased in St Paul's Building on Broadway and A. E. Parker was engaged as the Resident Manager. Parker was given a five-year contract, a salary of £360 per annum, and 10 per cent of the branch profits.

In 1913 other offices were opened in Chicago and Washington, DC. The Chicago office was located in the Monadnock Building and supervised by J. H. West, who had passed his qualifying examinations in London in 1911. The Washington office was managed by Herbert Kerslake, who, as has been mentioned, was sent out from the Birmingham office. Both men were given five-year contracts similar to A. E. Parker's, and by the end of 1914 net profits from the US operations amounted to $18,387.

Shortly after World War I another office was opened in San Francisco, and Marks & Clerk became the recognized specialists in North America for securing foreign patents for domestic attorneys, and American patents for foreign attorneys. They took instructions for obtaining patents for American inventions all over the world

1. Applications for British Patents made by Marks & Clerk

	1910	*1911*	*1912*	*1913*
Birmingham	158	163	156	133
Manchester	55	76	75	75
London	444	403	418	466
USA	834	963	1005	1046
	1491	1565	1654	1720

2. Applications for Foreign Patents made by Marks & Clerk

	1910	*1911*	*1912*	*1913*
Birmingham	41	33	59	37
Manchester	30	47	19	34
London	725	708	671	799
USA	210	538	830	1258
	1006	1345	1590	2140

3. Applications to and from Germany made by Marks & Clerk

	1910	*1911*	*1912*	*1913*
To Germany	138	186	224	283
From Germany	259	277	277	301
	347	463	501	584
Grand Totals:	2894	3373	3745	4444

and, reciprocally, they received instructions from foreign patentees
wishing to file applications with the US Patent Office. By the
mid-1920s they were one of the largest firms in the world specializing
in this type of work.

Germany also proved to be a fruitful source of business, and in
June 1913 Marks & Clerk opened an office in Berlin, with Hermann
Funke as Manager. Although business declined dramatically upon
the outbreak of hostilities in August 1914, the German authorities
did not force the closure of the Berlin office until 1917, and Herr
Funke was allowed to travel freely between London and Berlin.
After the War, the office was never re-opened.

Before closing this chapter, mention must be made of some of
the young men whom Sir George took under his wing as articled
clerks. All passed their qualifying examinations whilst in his

Family scene at St Bernards, Caterham.

employ, but for various reasons they do not feature elsewhere in our story.

Albert Mathys was born in 1876 and qualified in 1905. One suspects that, due to the lack of Partnership opportunities within Marks & Clerk, he left to establish his own practice in 1910. He became greatly respected within the profession, and in the years 1935 to 1947, served as a Council Member of the Chartered Institute of Patent Agents. In 1903 he married a Marks & Clerk employee, and their son also qualified as a Patent Agent. In due course, the son became Deputy Chairman of Courtaulds Ltd, a member of the Banks Committee, Chairman of the Standing Advisory Committee on Patents, and Chairman of the Government Commission on Trade Mark Law Revision. He was knighted in 1974 for his public services.

John Gray qualified in 1902 at the age of twenty-six. He managed the Manchester office successfully for some years, and left to take over the Patent and Trade Mark Department at British Thomson Houston Ltd, becoming a Director of this famous heavy electrical engineering company in 1927. He served on the Council of the Chartered Institute of Patent Agents from 1917 to 1923. Henry

Gruning qualified a year after Gray, and remained with Marks & Clerk until his retirement in 1938. He became a profit-sharing Partner in 1928, but for personal reasons declined the offer of a renewal of his Partnership in 1931. William Bryson qualified in 1906, and remained with the firm until 1914. After military service he set up on his own account and successfully ran his own business until his death in 1947.

Both R. F. Hargreaves and H. A. Smith, who qualified in 1907 and 1909 respectively, later joined Haseltine Lake & Company, London-based Patent Agents, and both eventually became Partners in the firm. Joseph Hubers qualified in 1908, and almost immediately set up his own practice, but unfortunately died prematurely in 1912. Finally, there was Charles Crompton, who commenced his articles in Birmingham, later transferring to London, where he qualified in 1910. Two years later he was appointed assistant to A. E. Parker in New York where he remained for the rest of his life.

Chapter 6

The Partnership (1914–1938)

The Earl of Stockton (then Mr Harold Macmillan) wrote in his autobiography, *Winds of Change*, 'The First War in contrast to the Second, burst like a bomb-shell upon ordinary people. It came suddenly and unexpectedly – a real "Bolt from the blue". Certainly, had we been told, when we were enjoying the carefree life of Oxford in the summer term of 1914, that in a few weeks all our little band of friends would abandon for ever academic life and rush to take up arms, still more, that only a few were destined to survive a four years' conflict, we should have thought such prophecies the ravings of a maniac.'

The indications are that Sir George Marks was uncertain about the need to go to war until the moment of the Declaration in spite of being a respected international businessman having close ties with Germany, and an experienced Member of Parliament belonging to the ruling party. The majority of his colleagues in the Liberal Party believed that Britain could and should keep out of the war unless directly attacked. Immediately war became a reality, Sir George, like tens of thousands of his fellow countrymen, placed himself at his country's service.

The British were slower than the Germans in awakening to the scale of munition supply required for trench warfare. Additionally, deliveries began to fall behind contract dates owing largely to the handicaps imposed by trade union rules on the dilution of skilled labour. Modification of the rules was only possible after protracted negotiation and the shortage of skills became so acute in the spring of 1915 as to lead to a public outcry. The outcome was the establishment of the Ministry of Munitions under Lloyd George, to co-ordinate and develop the supply and manufacture of raw materials.

Sir George Marks joined the new Ministry and was appointed Commissioner for Labour for the Newcastle-upon-Tyne district, responsible for the dilution of labour. This was a vitally important area for the war effort, since it included Sir W. G. Armstrong's giant Elswick Works, and the huge Vickers complex which produced big naval guns and the heaviest pieces of artillery. Sir George's first action in taking up his appointment is best told in his own words, for they illustrate his clear thinking and practical approach to all that he undertook in life. He was never afraid of being forthright and outspoken when the situation demanded.

I asked the men's leaders to meet me, and explained that we had not got enough men to get the ships out, to get the shells out, and the fuses out, and the grenades out, and a host of other things required for the war effort. I asked them to let me put in women. I explained that I was an engineer and that there were jobs I could have done just as well in the first week of my apprenticeship, as at the end of seven years, and that I wanted women and others to come in to do these easy jobs in order to stop the skilled men wasting their time. The trade union leaders thought that would never do. That would break down trade union organisation. The men would never stand it. I then said to them, 'Look here we are at war. Don't talk to me about your trade union organisation. Think about your country that is going through hell at the present time, and what you are doing. What are the men doing in the trenches out there? They do not think of their trades or even their lives. Get me the men you represent, and they won't say what you have said or I am deceived.' They still insisted the men wouldn't stand it.

I then asked which was the biggest room in Newcastle-upon-Tyne, the building holding the most people. They said the Grand Theatre. I picked up the telephone, and said to the Manager, 'I am the Commissioner and want your theatre tomorrow for a meeting at three o'clock.' The Manager protested that they had a matinee, to which I replied, 'Cut out the matinee, I am going to have a meeting. The Chief Constable of Newcastle will be there to see that I have a meeting.' A notice was put up in every works, that any man desiring to hear His Majesty's Commissioner explain the position could do so simply by notifying his foreman. Although these fellows had been working nights, Sundays and long hours overtime, and it was a fine chance for them to get a holiday, and although the building only held 8,000 people, 32,000 applied for leave to attend and we were packed out.

I insisted that it should be a men's meeting and that no employers and no managers should be present, and one of their leaders took the chair. Every man was called upon to show his union card and we cleared out everybody except trade unionists. I told my story and what we wanted to do and said that the Prime Minister in London was awaiting their reply, in order to know whether this great crowd of men was going to stand out as trade unionists first and foremost or as men willing to fight for their country. It was put to the meeting, and out of that great audience, 600 hands only were held up against my proposals. We carried on in Newcastle-upon-Tyne throughout the whole of the war without a strike, without an hour's cessation, with thousands of women and physically unfit men, who never before had been in a workshop. Unskilled and inefficient many may have been, but the materials so desperately needed by the fighting men flowed to the front as never before. The men I addressed that day were right at heart, but their leaders either didn't know it, or were afraid they would lose their jobs if they gave way to something that looked like a breakdown in trade union organisation.

The results of Sir George's action quickly spread throughout the country and the problem of dilution of labour was largely solved for the great good of the nation. In 1916 Sir George was appointed to make certain unspecified enquiries abroad upon behalf of the Ministry of Munitions, and shortly after the cessation of hostilities he was awarded the CBE for his work in the Ministry.

Dugald Clerk made an equally important contribution to the war effort, but in an academic rather than an organizational rôle. In 1916 he was appointed Director of Engineering Research at the Admiralty, and served on a number of advisory committees. The scientific work he co-ordinated and supervised whilst at the Admiralty was an important factor in the defeat of the German U-boat menace, which at once stage threatened to starve the British people into submission. Later he became a Member of the Advisory Committee for Aeronautics at the Air Ministry and Chairman of its International Combustion Engine Committee. He served also as a Member of the Air Inventions Committee. In 1917 he was knighted for his services, and made a KBE. Towards the end of the War the problems of water resources and the potential uses of water power began to interest him. The Conjoint Board of Scientific Societies invited him to become Chairman of its Water Resources Committee, and the Board of Trade appointed him to their Water Power Resources Committee. Later he wrote an important work, entitled *Water Power in the British Empire*, which was published by Constable & Co. in 1922.

Edward Marks was not directly involved in the war, quietly assuming overall responsibility for the day-to-day management of the Partnership in its entirety. In the months following the Declaration of War he established a testing and research laboratory at the Temple Street, Birmingham, offices, appointing J. D. Morgan as Superintendent. It was equipped with the latest types of measuring instruments and a wide range of apparatus for conducting investigations into the physical and electrical branches of applied science.

Dr John David Morgan, D.Sc., was a remarkable man born in 1879. He joined Marks & Clerk in 1896, passing his qualifying examinations as a Patent Agent in 1903. He was the author of many books and technical papers, perhaps his best known being *Principles of Ignition*. Throughout the War he worked closely with Joseph Lucas at the Temple Street Laboratory developing improved aircraft magnetos. He was considered an expert in many other fields, including the problems of mine damp explosions and the operation of submarines. His advice was sought by many prominent companies and other technical bodies. He was made a profit-sharing Partner in 1928, but became somewhat eccentric in later life. During the last twenty years of his life he attended neither the office nor Partnership meetings, confining his work to the drafting of Provisional Patent Specifications at the rate of one per day. The only help he would accept was from G. W. Rogers, an unqualified assistant sent down from London in 1936. Rogers dealt with the final specifications and all official correspondence, but was himself eventually forced to resign following a mental breakdown. Morgan died in March 1961 aged 82.

We saw in Chapter 3 that British Patent Law had been allowed to evolve by stages, rather than by sudden and drastic change. The first post-war Parliament lost no time dealing with further small, but notable, steps forward. The Patents and Designs Act 1919 introduced what were called 'Licences of Right'. Henceforth, a patentee could request that his patent was endorsed in accordance with the provisions of the Act and any person was then entitled to a licence to work the patent upon terms to be agreed between the two parties. In the event of failure to agree terms, the matter was settled by the Comptroller of Patents. The same Act also required the Comptroller to grant a licence to any applicant for patents relating to the preparation or production of food or medicine. In settling the terms between the parties the Comptroller was required to pay due regard to the desirability of food and medicine being available to the public at the lowest price possible consistent with giving the inventor his due reward for the research leading to the invention.

Sir George Marks was universally regarded as the leading authority in the House of Commons on all matters relating to Patent and Trade Mark Law. He made important contributions to

Dr John Morgan, D.Sc.

this Act and subsequent legislation both on the floor of the House and in the committee stages. However, in 1922, he and his three colleagues took a step which surprised their contemporaries in the profession by resigning *en bloc* from the Chartered Institute of Patent Agents following the passing of a new bye-law prohibiting advertising. In a protest speech Sir George claimed he was thinking primarily of Fellows wishing to start in practice upon their own account, as five of his assistants had done. He quoted often the cliché, 'A man who doesn't advertise his products or services is like a man winking at a girl in the dark – he knows what he is doing, but she doesn't!' Not until after Sir George's death in 1938 did the Partners rejoin the Chartered Institute.

In 1916 the Partnership capital stood at £38,349, thereafter until 1923 with declining income and profits due to the War and its aftermath, the Partners were compelled to draw upon their capital. Although business began to improve in 1919, recovery was slow. Trade generally was disappointing, many valuable export markets had been lost, and there was a good deal of industrial unrest at home. Lloyd George's promise of a 'land fit for heroes' failed to materialize. In 1923, at least so far as Marks & Clerk were concerned, the position stabilized, and the Partnership capital was restored to £44,279. During the next five years until Edward Marks's untimely death in 1928, at the age of fifty-two, the capital increased by over 50 per cent to £67,795.

The year 1923 also saw the unveiling of a memorial erected at 57–58 Lincoln's Inn Fields to the memory of the eight members of the staff who were killed during World War I. The plaque was inscribed with the following names:

S. F. Drake	T. V. Dunlop	C. W. H. Foord
E. W. B. Hogg	F. V. Loveday	I. F. Lowe
	C. Paterson	W. E. Uglow

By the end of 1925 the business had grown to such proportions that the Partners resolved formally to establish a second line of management comprising the following eight qualified assistants. Henry Dod was born in 1873 and passed his qualifying examinations in 1903. He shared with Dr Hettinger responsibility for the European and Translation Departments at Lincoln's Inn Fields for many years. He died in 1955. Henry Gruning has already been mentioned in the last chapter. Dr John Hettinger, Ph.D., was born in Rumania in 1880, passing his qualifying examinations and acquiring British Nationality in 1914. He became an authority on psychic phenomena and was author of an academic work on the subject entitled, *The Ultra-Perceptive Faculty*. Vivian Arthur Beesley Hughes, born in 1886, joined Marks & Clerk in 1901 and qualified in 1909. In later life he became Senior Partner at the Manchester office and a Director of the Chloride Electrical Storage Company. He played an important part in the development of man-made fibres and was responsible for the original Terylene patents. The rôle played by the brilliant Dr John Morgan has already been described.

The sixth member of the Executive, Percy Rayner-Smith, was

Percy Rayner-Smith.

born in 1884, joined Marks & Clerk in 1905 and qualified in 1912. At one stage he was employed by Sir Dugald Clerk's and Matthew Atkinson Adam's Consultancy Partnership. Later he was engaged in the litigation work conducted by Adam at Featherstone Buildings. In 1961 he became the Senior Partner of Marks & Clerk, retiring in 1972. He died in January 1974. William Triggs, CBE, was born in New Zealand in 1884. He joined Marks & Clerk in 1909 and qualified in 1921. He became highly respected in the profession and became a Council Member of the Chartered Institute of Patent Agents in 1940. In 1944–45 and again in 1949–50 he became its President. He was Master of the Inventions Lodge and succeeded Lord Marks as Senior Partner of Marks & Clerk following the latter's death in 1938. Before and during World War II he handled the patent work originating in the Cavendish Laboratory, Cambridge, where the first atom was successfully split, thereby laying the foundations of the present-day atomic energy industry. After the War he was responsible for a publication issued by the Chartered Institute commenting on the Patents Act 1949. He attended the important British Commonwealth Conference on Patents and Trade Marks in 1955. Without prior notice he suddenly announced his retirement in January 1961 and went to live in Denmark, where he died six years later. Finally, the eighth member, Robert Angus Wolstenholme, was born in 1887 and qualified as a Patent Agent in 1910. He devoted the whole of his working life to the firm based at Lincoln's Inn Fields, and was a full profit-sharing Partner for thirty-six years. Upon the retirement of William Triggs in 1961 he assumed the rôle of Deputy Senior Partner, taking over the responsibility for administering the London Office, deferring to Rayner-Smith on matters such as chairing meetings. He introduced the concept of managing the London Office with the assistance of a small committee of Partners. The names of all the members of the Executive were listed on the firm's notepaper in alphabetical order, and it was agreed that twelve months' notice of termination of employment was required on both sides.

Until the passing of the Patent Law Amendment Act of 1852, England, Scotland and Ireland each required separately filed patents. After this date patents filed at the Patent Office were recognized throughout Great Britain and Ireland. In 1925, following Independence, the Eire Government once again started issuing its own patents requiring registration in Dublin. In November that year Marks & Clerk opened an office at 4 Palace Street in the centre of Dublin, and appointed Wilfred Parker as Manager. Due to insufficient business the office was closed ten months later and the firm's interests in Eire were taken over by G. M. Cruickshank, a former Marks & Clerk employee.

In July 1928 the Partners were shocked by the news of the death of Edward Marks at the Kingsthorpe Nursing Home in Birmingham. Sir George was especially distressed and despondent, because the two brothers had always been absolutely devoted to each other. His first comment upon hearing the news was, 'I have lost my brakes!' Edward left an estate of £50,935 net and was survived by his wife, Lily, for only eighteen months. She was described as a melancholy person, having a habitual tendency to sadness and could not face life without her beloved Edward. She died peacefully in January 1930 at their home, 'Clydesdale', in Richmond Hill Road, Edgbaston, which they had acquired shortly after the War.

Within a few weeks of Edward's death the remaining Partners decided to dissolve the Executive established in 1925, and its members, with the exception of Henry Gruning, were made profit-sharing Partners in the firm. This was undoubtedly an extremely important and wise decision, and one which provided continuity of management for the next thirty years. The transformation from a successful four-man team, to a major international operation was completed, with a dozen highly qualified, experienced Partners working on both sides of the Atlantic.

World War I had ended with the American operation in good order. In 1919 fees charged in the United States amounted to $547,292, producing a net profit of $88,054, of which $56,172 was transferred to the London Bank account. With the dollar standing at $4.54 to the pound Sterling, this represented a welcome addition of £12,370 to the Partnership funds. A. E. Parker was given a new fourteen-year contract as Resident Manager of the New York office, which generated more than half the US profits, and in 1920 James Newton, formerly US Commissioner of Patents, was engaged to supervise Marks & Clerk's over-all operations in the United States. He received a salary of $8000 per annum and 1 per cent of net profits over $60,000, and 2 per cent of profits over $96,000. Messrs Highfield and Starling were sent out from London to strengthen the New York office team, but unfortunately Starling's wife died suddenly in 1922, and he elected to return to London. Joseph Fleming and George Wilson were sent out to replace him. In September 1920 an office was opened in the Crocker Building in San Francisco. J. S. Cole, another London assistant, was appointed Manager, and given a ten-year contract together with a salary of $2800 per annum and 20 per cent of the net profits of the branch. Shortly after Cole's arrival in San Francisco, Marks & Clerk acquired the firm Jackson & Webster and merged it with their new West Coast operation.

Undoubtedly, from the beginning, the sheet anchor of Marks & Clerk's American operation had been Sir George Marks's relationship with Thomas Elva Edison. Born in 1847, in a humble home in Ohio, Edison became one of the most extraordinary and brilliant men that America has produced. He started life as a train boy selling newspapers and candy on the Grand Trunk Railway. His introduction into the world of telecommunications came by accident. He had the good fortune to rescue a railway employee's

Thomas Alva Edison. A signed photograph presented to Lord Marks in September 1905.

child from being run down by a train, and the grateful father offered to teach him to operate the railway telegraph. Edison proved an apt pupil and soon obtained a position as an operator, but he was a restless, ambitious youth and found the work monotonous. He eventually found his way to Boston, where he resolutely applied himself to the study of science, and at the age of twenty-one obtained a post with the Gold & Stock Telegraph Company in New York. Whilst with them he developed his first important invention, the Stock Printer. This was quickly followed by other inventions in the field of applied electricity, and before long the Company offered him £8000 for his inventions. With this money he built his first workshop and from that point his career was an almost unbroken success.

Initially he concentrated upon improvements in the working of telegraphs and telephones. Later he turned his attention to the incandescent lamp and the phonograph, the forerunner of the gramophone. He undertook also important work associated with electric traction and pioneered a means whereby low-grade ores would be economically processed utilizing new magnetic techniques.

The development of the incandescent lamp took place simultaneously on both sides of the Atlantic. In 1879, Joseph Swan, working in Newcastle-upon-Tyne, demonstrated before his friend, Colonel R. E. Crompton, one of the pioneers of the electric generator, a row of twenty small incandescent lamps burning brightly and giving a steady, constant light. Swan was endeavouring to overcome the disadvantages of the earlier carbon arc lamp, and he concentrated on the development of a satisfactory means of exhausting the glass globes of the lamp, and new materials for the filament. He utilized a cotton thread for the latter, partially converting it into cellulose by immersion in sulphuric acid and then carbonizing it. Unknown to Swan, Edison arrived at a similar solution by a somewhat different route, and in 1881 took steps to patent his work, which had the effect of blocking the British invention. Swan then patented further improvements, and after legal arguments, the two men decided to pool their work. The Edison & Swan United Electric Light Company Ltd was founded in 1883, and for a time the two men enjoyed a worldwide monopoly manufacturing electric light bulbs.

In the late 1880s, what became known as the 'Battle of the Systems' reached its climax. On one side were the exponents of the direct current system of electricity supply, based on a series of small local generating stations such as were being established by many municipal authorities. Their opponents favoured the high-pressure alternating current mains supply originating in a small number of large power stations. The battle raged on both sides of the Atlantic simultaneously, and many distinguished engineers publicly took sides in favour of one system or the other. In Great Britain the champion of the AC system was the redoubtable Sebastian Ziani de Ferranti, who later became an important Marks & Clerk client. In the United States this system was advocated by George Westinghouse, the inventor of the automatic air-brake used extensively by the world's railways, and founder of the giant Westinghouse Electric Corporation. Thomas Edison led the opposition in the United States, and it seems probable that his international reputation contributed to the initial successes of the supporters of the DC system in the United Kingdom.

Edison first consulted Sir George Marks concerning his inventions in 1890, and for over twenty-five years Marks acted as his personal attorney, supervising his European interests. In 1911, much to the delight of Marks & Clerk's staff, the 'Wizard', as Edison became widely known, visited Lincoln's Inn Fields. A genuine friendship had developed between the two men, and Sir George became one of the comparatively few who enjoyed Edison's complete confidence.

It was in the field of the phonograph, and later the gramophone, that Sir George's relationship with Edison developed beyond that of attorney, patent agent and friend. For many years Sir George was Chairman of the Edison Phonograph Company in the United Kingdom. Later, in 1917, he was invited to join the Board of the Columbia Graphophone Company, a major company established to capitalize upon Edison's phonograph patents. In 1931, when the company merged with its major competitor, the American-owned Gramophone Company (HMV), he was its Chairman. But that story belongs to the next chapter.

Throughout the 1920s, in spite of his heavy commitments at Lincoln's Inn Fields, in America and as a member of the House of Commons, Sir George undertook limited assignments as a Consulting Engineer. His advice was sought in connection with improvements to Torquay and Bude harbours, and for some years he and Lady Marks enjoyed a holiday home named 'Panarvor' at Bude. Annually they entertained Edward Marks's family and Lady

'Panarvor', Lord Marks's holiday home at Bude in north Cornwall.

Marks's brothers and sisters and their children. In 1922 Sir George was consulted by Torquay Corporation regarding a proposal to build a Cliff Railway at Babbacombe on the eastern outskirts of the town. The 750-ft-long line, laid to a gradient of 1 in 2.84, was eventually built by his old competitor, R. Waygood Ltd, for the National Electric Construction Company. It was completed at a cost of over £15,000 and opened to the public in 1926. Traction was provided for the two cable-hauled cars by an 85 b.h.p. 300 volts direct current electric motor. When the electric tramways were abandoned in 1934, the railway was acquired by Torquay Corporation, who continued to operate it until the War forced its temporary closure in 1941. After the War it was substantially rebuilt and modernized and re-opened to the public in 1951. In recent years it is said to have carried some 800,000 passengers annually.

In the years following World War I, Padstow on the North Cornish coast became one of the chief fishing ports in the West Country. It had been a port since the thirteenth century, but in the 1920s the East Coast trawlermen began using it extensively during the Spring fishing season. The port was the most westerly point on the old London & South Western Railway, which became a port of the Southern Railway in the 1923 Grouping. That year Padstow despatched by rail 40,000 cases of fish weighing 2500 tons, and over 7000 tons of bunkering coal for the fifty-two trawlers using the port and 500 tons of ice were received by rail. Such was the new-found prosperity of the town that the population increased by some 500 persons.

Sir George Marks was appointed Engineer to the Padstow Harbour Commissioners, and he immediately put in hand major improvements to the berthing arrangements and other facilities required by the trawlermen and railway company. When proposals for further extending the harbour were introduced, Edward Marks was appointed Consulting Engineer. The project aroused considerable interest amongst civil engineers generally, because of the many unique problems involved in the scheme. In spite of opposition from certain quarters, Edward advocated the extensive use of ferro-concrete but, unfortunately, he died before his scheme was completed.

The project was revived in 1930, and a proposal to construct a new breakwater at the harbour entrance was promoted by Sir Donald MacLean, Sir George's successor as MP for the North Cornwall constituency. It was estimated that the scheme would cost £40,000, but neither the Harbour Commissioners nor the Southern Railway felt able to provide the finance. A local landowner, Colonel C. R. Prideaux-Brune, agreed to donate the quarried stone required, and Sir George Marks offered his professional services free, but the work was never wholly completed.

Sir George's final act of generosity towards the people of Padstow took place in 1934, when he purchased a piece of land at Mount Pleasant from Prideaux-Brune. He donated this to the townspeople and had a shelter erected for their comfort and pleasure.

Sir Dugald Clerk and Matthew Atkinson Adam continued to enhance their reputations as Consultants and Expert Witnesses throughout the 1920s, and both were honoured by various professional bodies. The academic world paid its tribute too, and the Universities of Glasgow, Leeds, Liverpool, Manchester and St

The Babbacombe cliff railway, Torquay, to which Lord Marks acted as a consultant during the early planning and design stages.

Andrews awarded Sir Dugald honorary degrees. He became a member of the University Grants Committee, Chairman of the Delegacy of the City & Guilds Engineering College and Prime Warden of the Goldsmiths Company.

In 1920 the Institution of Gas Engineers elected Sir Dugald as its President. Although not strictly speaking a professional gas engineer, he had been an honorary member of the Institution since 1908. In his Presidential Address he referred at length to pending legislation which would, 'enable the gas industry to settle for itself, by the introduction of improved methods of gas production, the exact nature of the modified processes to be employed to supply the public with the gas best suited to produce heat, power and light at the lowest practicable price, and the maximum economy in coal'. This legislation, The Gas Regulation Act 1920, introduced thermal units as the basis of charging and the well-known 'therm', which is equivalent to 100,000 B.Th.U.s, became established. Later Sir Dugald presented another important paper before the Institution, entitled 'The Relevant Thermal Value of Gas & Electricity'.

Another appointment which gave Sir Dugald considerable pleasure was the two years he served as Chairman of the Council of the Royal Society of Arts, which culminated in him being awarded the Society's coveted Albert Medal. During the same period he also served as a Council Member of the Royal Society. In 1932 he was elected President of the Institution of Civil Engineers, but sadly failing health prevented him taking office. His wife, Margaret, had died in September 1930, and thereafter Sir Dugald appeared to lose interest in his many outside activities. On 12 November 1932 he died quietly at his home, 'Lukyns', at Ewhurst in Surrey, leaving an Estate valued at £54,412.

Politically his sympathies had always been with the Liberal Party, and he keenly supported his friend and Partner Sir George Marks's political activities. He devoted most of his leisure to writing, and one of his last books was a work entitled, *The Works & Discoveries of Joule*, based on the famous English physicist's work. He remained an active supporter of the Royal Automobile Club and the Royal Clyde Yacht Club until his death. He and his wife never lost their love for the River Clyde, and they returned to Helensburgh as often as possible. For many years he was a member of both the Reform Club and the Athenaeum. The majority of his reports and papers were deposited in the Kensington Science Museum and at the Smithsonian Museum in Washington, DC. In 1972 his extensive library was presented to the Science Museum by Marks & Clerk.

Upon the Bicentenary of the birth of James Watt in 1936, the Institution of Mechanical Engineers established the James Watt International Gold Medal. This award is bestowed every two years on an engineer of any nationality deemed to merit the highest award the Institution can confer or that a mechanical engineer can receive. Representative engineering societies throughout the world are invited to submit their recommendations to the Council of the

Robert Angus Wolstenholme.

Institution, who make the final choice. This meritorious scheme was made possible by a £2000 legacy bequeathed by Sir Dugald Clerk. In deciding who should be the recipient of the first award, the Council thought that it would be appropriate on this occasion, that the claims of railway engineers should be given a special priority. The Institution had originated amongst railway men, and George Stephenson, the most famous of them all, had been its first President. It was felt that in view of his seniority and standing in the profession, the honour should fall upon Sir John Aspinall, the former Chief Mechanical Engineer of the Lancashire & Yorkshire Railway. By a strange quirk of fate Sir John died only three days before the Medal was to have been publicly presented to him.

In 1933 the effects of the economic recession were being widely felt throughout industry and commerce. The number of British and foreign patents filed that year showed a dramatic decline when compared with previous years, and the Partners decided to terminate the profit-sharing element in the 1928 Partnership Agreement. In April a new deed was signed, listing the following Partners: Sir George Croydon Marks, Sir Dugald Clerk, M. A. Adam, H. E. Dod, J. Hettinger, V. A. B. Hughes, J. D. Morgan,

William Warren Triggs, CBE

P. Rayner-Smith, W. W. Triggs, and R. A. Wolstenholme. Although the Partners were listed in alphabetical order on the firm's stationery, W. W. Triggs was in fact the largest shareholder. It was further agreed that J. I. Newton, the former US Commissioner of Patents, who had been retained to supervise the firm's North American operations, should in future attend London Partners' meetings, and that written minutes of such meetings should be maintained.

Two years later the Partners agreed to take out life insurance to provide collateral for loans which it was necessary to raise from time to time as additional working capital was required. They were anxious also to be in a position at all times adequately to remunerate Sir George Marks, as Governor and General Manager of the firm. Sir George, now a comparatively wealthy man, took this opportunity of himself offering to subscribe any additional cash required by the Partnership, as an alternative to seeking new Bank borrowing facilities.

A new Patents Act reached the Statute Book in 1932, and that year Sir George Marks and R. A. Wolstenholme published a widely acclaimed 'White Book' entitled, *The Patents & Design Acts, 1907–1932*, which remained a standard work of reference for many years. Two years later the Institute of Trade Mark Agents was incorporated, and Sir George was invited to become its first President, an honour which he declined, stating that he felt that the appointment should go to a younger man. However, he remained keenly interested in maintaining and developing the high standards of the profession, and the first Trade Mark Agents' examinations, held in 1935, actually took place in his Lincoln's Inn Fields flat.

Every year several articled clerks and assistants employed by Marks & Clerk successfully sat their examinations for membership of the Chartered Institute of Patent Agents, and a number subsequently filled distinguished appointments in the profession. John Farrer was a typical candidate, passing his qualifying examinations in 1924. Subsequently he left Marks & Clerk to become a Partner in Page, White & Farrer. He was elected to the Council of the Chartered Institute of Patent Agents in 1942 and became its President in 1950–51. He was for many years closely associated with the Yeomanry, and was a keen sportsman and rugby footballer. He played a prominent rôle in the Rugby Union Referees' Association. Another successful candidate was Frederick Crockett who qualified in 1929, and in due course became head of the Patent Department of Electrical & Musical Industries Ltd (EMI), a company with which Sir George Marks was closely associated from its formation. Frank Foxton left Marks & Clerk in 1941 to join the Ministry of Supply, having qualified in 1931. Subsequently he had a distinguished career with the Atomic Energy Authority. Dr George Frazer, a graduate of Liverpool University, was employed at the Manchester office when he qualified as a Patent Agent in 1935. In due course he emigrated to Australia, where he acquired the practice of Griffith, Hassel & Frazer. Later he qualified as a Patent Attorney and became President of the Australian Institute of Patent Attorneys.

Throughout the 1930s the provincial branch offices continued to make satisfactory contributions to the partnership profits. The Birmingham office, under the control of Dr John Morgan, removed to 7 Newhall Street in 1929, and in 1936 it again moved to larger, more prestigious, premises in Lombard House, Great Charles Street. George Cruickshank, assisted by C. C. Gall, continued to run both the Glasgow and Dublin offices. In 1932 they acquired the

Glasgow practice of W. R. M. Thomson & Co., following the death of the proprietor. In similar circumstances the firm of J. Liddle was purchased in 1934 and both firms were amalgamated in the St Vincent Street offices in May 1937.

Sir George, now Lord Marks, continued to make regular visits to North America during the first half of the 1930s. Frequently he combined his business activities with political and other official engagements and always derived enormous personal pleasure from these visits. He had made many friends in both the United States and Canada, and in a sense became an ambassador extraordinary in matters of trade and patent law.

The firm's first branch office in Canada was opened at 128 Wellington Street, Ottawa, in 1921 under the supervision of Richard Jarvis, who had been sent out from London. In 1924 control passed to Alex McRae, with Jarvis remaining as Assistant Manager. A second Canadian office opened in 1930 at 320 Bay Street, Toronto, under the supervision of McRae's brother. Unfortunately, two years later McRae resigned following a dispute with the United Kingdom partners, and set up on his own account, taking the majority of Marks & Clerk's clients with him. J. S. Cole was transferred from the New York office to take charge of the Canadian operation, but the situation remained difficult and in due course the Toronto business was sold. Later, following the tragic death of Cole from arsenical poisoning, Jarvis was reinstated as Manager of the Ottawa office.

Marks & Clerk's performance in the United States during the 1920s was good. In the ten-year period 1921–30 annual fees charged to clients increased from $526,800 to $1,083,900 and many significant patents were handled by the firm. Lord Marks's old-fashioned British charm and his extrovert personality were much admired by the Americans, which, combined with the expert local knowledge of James Newton, provided the cornerstones of Marks & Clerk's success in the New World. The New York office always provided the greater proportion of the revenue earned, with the Washington office second and Chicago third.

Unfortunately A. E. Parker, the Manager of the New York office, was taken seriously ill in 1926, and was replaced by Walter Pearson, another British Patent Agent sent out from London. Parker had played a major rôle in the development of the branch since it opened in 1910, and was sorely missed by the firm. Two years later

George Wilson, who had been at the New York office since 1922, took over as Manager of the San Francisco operation. In August 1930 the Partners decided to lease a prestigious twelve-room suite in the National Press Building in Washington, DC. Both James Newton and Herbert Kerslake had their offices in the suite, and Lord Marks used it extensively for lavish entertaining whenever he was visiting the United States. He became well known as a most affable host, and the younger members of his wife's family recall the stories he delighted telling of the distinguished and interesting people he had entertained.

The traumatic years following the Wall Street crash had their effect upon Marks & Clerk's North American business. The San Francisco office moved into a loss situation in 1931, and it was joined by the Chicago office in 1932. Net profits from the US operation that year amounted to only $23,250. In January 1933 the Partners in London decided that the Washington office should discontinue filing cases at the US Patent Office. Later, an established American firm, Glascock, Downing & Seebold, took over Marks & Clerk's filing practice. Initially it was agreed that part of the profits from this operation should go to the British Partners, but the arrangement broke down, due mainly to an accumulation of debts owed by German firms since World War I. These debts were eventually settled by the US Custodian of Enemy Property.

In March 1935 two misfortunes befell the firm. James Newton died, and J. H. West, who had opened the Chicago office in 1913, left Marks & Clerk to set up on his own account. Lord Marks was then in his seventy-seventh year and slowing down. The North American operations had always been very much his personal concern, and none of the other London Partners was sufficiently experienced or able to deal with the partial vacuum created by these events. Their reaction was to bring the United States and Canadian operations within the terms of the 1931 United Kingdom Partnership deed. For various reasons this arrangement proved unsatisfactory, and in August 1937 the first American Partnership was formed. The Partners were W. G. Pearson, New York; Herbert Kerslake, Washington; Byfleet Ravenscroft, Chicago; and G. W. Wilson, San Francisco. Shortly before Lord Marks's death in September 1938, he had the satisfaction of knowing that the annual turnover of the four U.S. branch offices had been restored to $574,844, producing a net profit of $41,611.

Chapter 7

George Croydon Marks –
Politician, Peer and Businessman

George Croydon Marks was forty-eight years old when he accepted an invitation to stand as Liberal candidate for the Launceston constituency at the forthcoming General Election. He had supported the Liberal cause all his adult life, and undoubtedly was encouraged to accept the nomination by his friend and mentor, Sir George Newnes, who had himself entered the House of Commons in 1885. The picture of Parliamentary life painted by Newnes appealed to George Marks, but perhaps even more than the allure of the personal advantages and honours to be gained, he was drawn by the visions which every enthusiast of his temperament has: dreams of serving his country, and his fellow-men, and of advancing causes that seemed good and great.

The seat had been previously held by Fletcher Moulton, a friend of Marks, who had recently been elevated to the House of Lords. The opposing Conservative candidate, George Sandys, was an extremely popular local figure, and many thought he would have little difficulty defeating the largely unknown engineer from London. Sandys had excellent credentials. He had been educated at Clifton College, and at Pembroke College, Cambridge. He was a Boer War veteran, and owner of the White Hart Hotel in Launceston, but his supporters under-estimated the potential of George Marks's personal charm and eloquent oratory. Free trade, amendments to the Education Act, the curtailment of wasteful Government expenditure, unemployment and the licensing laws were the main topics upon which Marks concentrated his spirited and determined campaign. The election took place on 20 January 1906, and Marks polled 4658 votes against his opponent's 2736, a majority of 1922. The new House of Commons met for the first time on 13 February with Sir Henry Campbell-Bannerman as Prime Minister.

In the Commons, Marks was generally a silent member, although always appearing cheerful and debonair, and a contemporary journalist described him as 'One of the most striking looking men in the House.' Somewhat surprisingly he apparently never made an outstanding speech in the House, and never introduced a political Bill. However, in spite of his many outside business commitments, he quickly established a reputation as an excellent constituency member and a staunch and loyal supporter of his Party. In the field of Patent Law and cognate subjects he became universally recognized as a leading expert and rendered much valuable service in Parliamentary committees.

His generous and conscientious service was soon rewarded by having the honour of a Knighthood conferred upon him on the occasion of King George V's Coronation. On 10 June 1911 he received a personal letter from Mr Asquith, the Prime Minister, informing him of the King's command, and on 6 July he went to St James's Palace to be dubbed by the King. A charming letter from Sir George, addressed to his niece, Ella Russell, remains extant and is reproduced in full:

London
July 6th 1911

My Dear Ella,

I daresay you will like to hear what happened to me this morning at St James's Palace, as it is not an everyday occurrence to just walk down to see the King and tell him you want to be Knighted and he does it and then all is over. Instead it is a very elaborate kind of display and is very awful in its formality.

I went in a taxi so that people should not see my cocked hat and my knickerbocker legs and sword, to St James's Palace getting there at to 11 when I had to give up my cocked hat in one of the halls and proceed through a line of very gorgeously dressed officials with plumed helmets and drawn swords to keep us in order, one white glove being worn by me on the left hand, but the right hand was naked. We were kept in different rooms, those who were to be K.C.B.'s were in one room, those who were to be other Knights in other rooms and Knights Bachelors in one very handsome apartment that looked out over a beautiful garden of the Palace in which were drawn up the Life Guards mounted, with their restive horses not liking the hot sun and the men and officers looking as though their plumes were very uncomfortable for them.

We waited in this room for about two hours, talking to each other and asking each other what we were to be called hereafter. Everybody seemed to think that I was going to be called 'Sir Croydon' as they said I had always been known as Croydon Marks but I explained that when they heard the King say something to me, they would find that it was 'George' and not 'Croydon', so that I should be

Sir George Croydon Marks, or Sir G. Croydon Marks when printed, and Sir George when spoken to. After this long wait an official read out the names and examined each card of those waiting, and then we went in alphabetical order through one beautiful room in which we were arranged like silken cords to form a kind of passage-way and along the cords here and there uniformed officers in full dress with drawn swords to keep us from running away if we got frightened. When we went through the first room we passed another room in which there was also a passage-way made with silken cords each gentleman as he passed carrying his card in his hand, and now and then, one of the officials looking at the card, and then looking at the name on the printed list to see that all was in order. Having got through these two approach rooms, we came to the third, or Presence Chamber. In this Presence Chamber was the King. At one end in the centre was a kind of semi-circle of officers and others about him, and immediately facing him the Gentlemen-at-Arms in their full uniform, while on each side were officers and others forming a lane through which we had to pass to the King. I gave up my card to one official, who looked at it and passed it to two or three others who in turn looked at it and it then went on to the Lord Chamberlain, who read out in a clear voice, 'Mr George Marks to receive the honour of Knighthood'. I was then standing in front of the King alone, and bowed low enough to look at the buttons on my waistcoat, that being the instruction. Having bowed, I knelt down on one knee on a cushion at the King's feet, the King standing the whole time. The Sword Bearer then gave the King the Sword and he tapped me on one shoulder first with the blade of the Sword and then lifted it over my head and tapped me on the other shoulder and then handed the Sword back to the officer. I then put my arm out as previously instructed with no glove upon my right hand, the arm resting as it were, horizontally in front of me about level with my chest. On my wrist the King placed his right hand which was ungloved, and I then had to raise his right hand to my lips and kiss it. While it was there at my lips the King said 'Rise, Sir George'. I got up, bowed again, and he bowed and smiled. I walked backwards taking care that the sword did not get in the way and then when I had got to the end of the semi-circle there was another gentleman in front of the King ready to be Knighted.

There were other officers and Ministers standing by the King, but I do not know who they were, for it seemed as though I could not see anyone but the King, and I found afterwards that others were in the same position. We were all too nervous, too tired or too frightened to see anybody else except the King. I walked outside into the vestibule; I got my cocked hat, and came away the ceremony being over. So far as Mr George Croydon Marks was concerned he was then officially dead and there was left in his shoes the man the King had called, 'Sir George'.

George Croydon Marks in his Knight's regalia.

Now isn't this quite a fairy tale! It was pretty yet it was very long and very shaking in its nerve effects. I spoke to an officer afterwards who told me that although he was a General, when he was in front of the King he felt like a subaltern.

Now best love to you, Arthur, Ralph, Father & Mother
Your affectionate Uncle

George.

Sir George and Lady Marks continued to devote as much time as possible to the Launceston constituency, residing at 'Panarvor', at nearby Bude. They were often accompanied by their young nieces and nephews on these visits, and always derived enormous pleasure from having young people around them.

In 1882, Lady Marks's younger sister, Martha Ann Maynard, had married Walter Pearce, a Bristol engineer, and they were blessed with ten children. At the turn of the century it was mutually agreed that their eldest daughter, Irene May, born in 1887, should become George and Maggie Marks's ward. They lavished great affection on the child, who was always known to members of the family as 'Queenie', and arranged for her education at Dr Williams's School, Dolgellau in North Wales. In 1912 Queenie married John Usher, the youngest son of Samuel Usher, and his second wife Anne. Usher was a manufacturing jeweller in Birmingham, a prominent member of the Congregational Church, and a close friend of George and Edward Marks since the time they were employed at Tangye's Cornwall Works.

The family were saddened by the deaths of William and Amelia Marks, Sir George's parents, during World War I. William, who was pre-deceased by Amelia, was 84 years old when he died in February 1918, still living in Myrtle Cottage, near his beloved church. He had retired from Woolwich Arsenal in 1898, having completed forty-three years' continuous service. Both he and Amelia were actively associated with the church Sunday School for over sixty years as teachers, secretary and superintendent. Although never financially well off and basically simple people, they were the 'salt of the earth', always offering help and friendship when it was needed, and setting a magnificent example to the young people in the district. They were for long affectionately remembered by many people in Eltham.

In 1917 Sir George further cemented his connection with his constituency by accepting an invitation to sit on the North Cornwall Bench, having retired from the Aberystwyth and Caterham Benches. Simultaneously he joined the Board of the British Equitable Assurance Company. From the moment he had put up his plate as a Consulting Engineer in Birmingham thirty years earlier, he had held an insurance agency, and felt completely at home in the Company's Boardroom. In 1924 the Guildhall Insurance Company acquired control of British Equitable, and four years later Sir George was appointed Chairman, a position he held until his death.

The Columbia Graphophone Company was founded to exploit commercially Edison's gramophone patents, and Sir George, as Chairman of Edison's United Kingdom Company, was a natural choice as a Director. Within a few years he became Chairman and presided over a period of rapid growth masterminded by his good friend and the Company's Chief Executive, Louis Sterling. During Sir George's Chairmanship the old-established Birmingham bicycle manufacturer Rudge Whitworth, whom he had acted for as a Patent Agent many years earlier, was acquired by Columbia. During this period Sir George also served on the Boards of a Cornish China Clay Company and a well-known manufacturer of cream custard.

In 1857, following an initiative by Sir Joseph Whitworth, the Institution of Mechanical Engineers passed a resolution whereby members pledged themselves to adopt the decimal system of measurement. However, over a century elapsed before decimalization became a reality. The Government's first action in the movement towards decimalization took place in 1918, when they set up a Royal Commission on Decimal Coinage. Sir George Marks was appointed a member of the Commission, which in due course published its findings, but nothing of significance happened for nearly forty years. In retrospect, it is extraordinary that Sir George was able to find the time to attend to so many responsibilities and varied interests simultaneously. He gave each his close personal attention and brought a high degree of professionalism to everything he undertook.

A General Election was held in 1918, and following some boundary changes, Launceston constituency became known as North Cornwall. Sir George, as might be expected, fought a vigorous campaign, concentrating on the many problems that were inevitably going to face a post-war Britain, and he regained his seat with a handsome majority. He was deeply concerned about the stance being taken by the workforce and by the thousands of men being demobilized from the armed forces. He saw the growing power and influence of the trade unions as a threat to the country's economic prosperity. It was as though he sensed a backlash following the overriding of organized labour attitudes and dogma during the War. He recalled his confrontation with the men's leaders in Newcastle-upon-Tyne, when he was Commissioner responsible for the dilution of labour, and was apprehensive about future industrial relations. He was in no doubt about the tremendous task which lay ahead if we were to regain lost export markets; he understood the strength of the competition, and realized that the mood of the working classes was that 'the world owed them a living'.

In one widely reported speech, he quoted from the scriptures, 'In the oldest book in the world, the divine command asserts – "Except a man work, he shall not eat". It is sometimes forgotten that that is a divine command. It is sometimes assumed that labour is a degradation instead of being an obligation.' In 1921, upon his twenty-first visit to Chicago, he warned his American audience of his concern. 'You in America should do everything possible to prevent the labour movement becoming a political movement. It is a mad, wrong thing, and it will be the undoing of you, if you do. There are men whose purpose is the upsetting of the present organization, and putting a worse one in its place.'

Sir George became a Member of the Council of the London Chamber of Commerce in 1924, and freely added his wisdom and experience to its deliberations. That year he led a Trade Delegation from the Chamber to Czechoslovakia, and returned convinced that the country was on the threshold of developing into a major industrial nation. He was especially impressed, and one suspects a little apprehensive, about all that he saw at the giant Skoda engineering and armaments factory.

Sir George's eighteen years in the House of Commons ended in 1924, defeated at the General Election by the Conservative candidate, Sir Donald MacLean. Although he was content to have more time to devote to Marks & Clerk and his other business commitments, he continued to provide an important behind-the-scenes link between the Liberal Party and Mr Ramsay MacDonald, the Leader of the Labour Party, with whom he had developed a close personal friendship. He welcomed also the opportunity of more travel, for he was always a great traveller, and now had the time to enjoy even more frequent visits to the United States and Canada.

The year 1929 saw the country plunged into economic and political crisis more serious than anything that had been known since the present Parliamentary system had been established. Trade everywhere was in recession, there was a run on the pound, and unemployment reached alarming proportions. In May, Sir George paid a short visit to Ottawa, only a few weeks before the great Wall Street crash, which caused even greater chaos to the American economy. He stayed with his former friend and colleague Lord Willingdon, the Governor General, who as Inigo Freeman-Thomas had been Liberal MP for Bodmin during the period Sir

George represented North Cornwall. As well as politics, the two men shared an interest in railways, for Lord Willingdon's grandfather was the celebrated pioneer railway contractor, Thomas Brassey. In an interview with the Press, given at the Governor General's residence, Sir George announced that he was definitely out of politics, and that he was lending his support to none of the political parties at home.

Later in the month a General Election was held, which the Conservatives lost, enabling Mr Ramsay MacDonald to form his second Labour Government, but the new Administration was at the mercy of fifty-five Liberal MPs. Upon his return home, Sir George Marks had a change of heart and he surprised many of his friends and former colleagues by announcing that he was leaving the Liberals and joining the Labour Party. On 22 June he declared, 'I believe in Mr Ramsay MacDonald entirely. I can see no reason at all why Liberals of my way of thinking should remain outside such important matters, when they could possibly be of great assistance in giving Mr MacDonald the support that he needs. There is no room for three political parties if stable Government is to be carried on.' Another secession which caused a great deal of comment and speculation at the time, was that of Sir William Jowitt, the former Attorney-General, and Liberal Member of Parliament for Preston. Sir George jumped to his defence, commenting, 'What Sir William Jowitt has done is entirely consistent with his attitude as a progressive Liberal.' Reflecting upon Sir George's defection one national daily newspaper reported, 'The Chairman of the Columbia Graphophone Company, a Liberal, has joined the Labour Party. Lloyd George has got the "NEEDLE".' Events moved quickly, and on 11 July 1929 it was announced to the *London Gazette* that Sir George Croydon Marks and Sir William MacKenzie had been elevated to the Peerage upon the recommendation of the new Prime Minister. Five days later Sir George declared, 'I have definitely returned to the political arena, and will take a regular part in the debates in the Upper House.' At the same time he made it known that he had chosen the title The First Baron Marks of Woolwich. On 18 July at 3.45 p.m. the Lord Chancellor took his seat on the Woolsack. Lord Marks, supported by Lord Parmoor and Lord Arnold, was introduced to the assembled Peers and took his seat. Twenty-five minutes later their Lordships rose. One wonders what thoughts went through the First Lord Marks of

Woolwich's mind during those twenty-five minutes. Although a leader of men, in some respects having the extrovert attributes of the showman, he was fundamentally a humble man and dedicated Christian. In the social sense he persistently kept out of the news. He was a very private person, and yet no one could wish to meet a more perfect host or a more entertaining guest. A man of seventy tends to remember details of his distant past more clearly than recent events and no doubt his childhood in Eltham, his apprenticeship at Woolwich Arsenal, his college days in London and his early career at Erith, in Dublin and at the Cornwall Works in Birmingham all crossed his mind, but one suspects a prayer of thanksgiving for his manifold blessings and good fortune was uppermost in his thoughts.

Shortly after his induction, with the aid of the College of Heraldry, he formalized and registered his Coat of Arms. He chose as his motto, 'Animo et Labore' – 'With Patience and Labour' – and in the quaint language of heraldry, his Coat of Arms was described in the following terms:

Arms — Argent on a chevron gules two martlets respectant or, on a chief sable a greyhound courant of the field.

Crest — A winged lion sejant gules resting the dexter paw on a closed book gold.

Supporters – On either side a winged lion rampant gules charged on the shoulder with an open book or.

In October 1929 Lord Marks accompanied the Prime Minister on a visit to Washington and Toronto. They crossed the Atlantic in the liner *Berengaria*, and undoubtedly a very close relationship between the two men was cemented during the voyage. In Washington Lord Marks told reporters, 'Mr Ramsay MacDonald comes not as a leader of any political party, but as the representative of all Britain. He comes to the United States to meet your officials as he would friends. His prime objective is to promote this spirit of friendship.' Perhaps surprisingly, in view of the acute economic crisis on both sides of the Atlantic, he added, 'Our main topic of conversation will be disarmament.' Upon their return home Lord Marks continued to fulfil the important rôle of providing a link between the Prime Minister and members of the Liberal Party, who still effectively held the balance of power in the House of Commons.

Lord Marks's coat of arms.

The following year Lord Marks was chosen to perform another pleasant duty as a member of the British Delegation to the celebrations marking the 1000th Anniversary of the founding of the Icelandic Parliament. The delegation was led by the Prime Minister and included in addition to Lord Marks, Lords Newton and Lamington, Sir Robert Hamilton, MP, and Mr Rhys Davies, MP. The British party sailed into Reykjavik Harbour on 26 June 1930 aboard the 35,000-ton battleship HMS *Rodney*, escorted by two Blackburn Iris flying boats. The King and Queen of Denmark, and the Crown Prince of Sweden were present at the three-day celebrations, which included an open-air session of the Althing, or Parliament, held in the presence of the majority of the island's population.

Following a grand banquet given by the Icelandic Government, Lord Marks made a speech in which he said, 'Iceland is an example of what the freedom of a people can do. The people of Iceland have taught us through 1000 years that the will of the people is the main point of statesmanship.'

By the end of the summer of 1930, with the unemployment problem dramatically worsening, the Government faced its most serious crisis. There was strongly marked disagreement in the Cabinet on fiscal, economic and other questions to be included in the new legislative programme to be tackled in the forthcoming Parliamentary Session. Lord Marks continued to play an important rôle maintaining the slender Liberal support for the Labour Government. He was rewarded by being invited to second Lord Sanderson's motion following the Opening of Parliament on 28 October.

In his humble address following the speech from the throne, Lord Marks expressed the delight of the House and the nation, that the King had fully recovered from a serious illness, and was once again able to take his place in the Chamber. He then went on to deal with the economic crisis, saying that, throughout the country all industries were depressed, because the spending power of the world had been lessened and that the fortunes of all industries and all nations were inextricably interrelated. He claimed that the United States, with which he was especially familiar, was suffering from the effects of the depression far more than Great Britain. He urged that the country must achieve better consolidation and better marketing of its products, and that some kind of counsel between employers and workmen was necessary if betterment was to be expected. He referred to the difficulty of the farmer. The farmer could not control the elements, which could make or mar his efforts. Therefore, it was essential that, as in manufacturing, so in farming, there should be consolidation. Improved transport, cheap handling, and not too many handlers, were needed if the situation were to be improved.

In the following months Lord Marks contributed significantly to the deliberations of the Upper House as it dealt with the controversial Glasgow Corporation Bill, the School Attendance Bill, Proportional Representation, and the Arab-Jewish question. He put up a strenuous fight on the omnibus powers portion of the Glasgow Corporation Bill, and was one of the fourteen Labour Peers who voted against the School Attendance Bill. Always a

Lord and Lady Marks in their peer's robes.

Liberal at heart, he supported proportional representation and pointed out the anomaly that 90,000 votes were cast at the last General Election to secure each Liberal seat, whereas only 20,000 to 30,000 votes were given in favour of each member representing the other two parties. Dealing with the Arab-Jewish question, he said that it was not merely a problem between Arabs and Jews, but that British honour was at stake in the search for a solution.

Later, in November 1931, when guest of honour at the 303rd Cutlers' Feast in Sheffield, Lord Marks amused his audience saying, 'The bulk of the work done in the House of Lords is done by those who have sat in the Commons, where they had learned to shed their bad manners.' Twelve months later, as the economic and

Warrant creating the first Baron Marks of Woolwich.

unemployment crisis continued to dominate affairs, he said of politicians, 'They are too much concerned about their own propaganda, rather than the material demands made upon them. The public do not want labels and propaganda. A great common leader is wanted today, who will bring together all men desiring to benefit the nation as a nation, and not a party machine. The nations of the world today are like a row of bricks waiting to see how long it will be before the next one falls.'

Following Stanley Baldwin's and the Conservatives' success at the polls, one suspects that Lord Marks became disillusioned and tired of politics. He was now seventy-five, living in Bournemouth and devoting the greater part of his time to philanthropic works and his garden. However, his close friendships with Ramsay MacDonald and his daughters continued, and it was with feelings of personal loss that he learned of the former Prime Minister's death at sea whilst on a cruise to South America. The body was returned to Plymouth aboard HMS *Apollo* and transferred to the Cornish Riviera express to Paddington, where Lord Marks awaited its arrival, prominent amongst the many waiting mourners.

Concurrently with events culminating in Lord Marks's elevation to the House of Lords, he was at the very centre of a take-over battle which caused a stir in financial circles on both sides of the Atlantic. In May 1929, whilst he was crossing the Atlantic in the Cunard liner *Aquitania*, en route to New York, rumours started to circulate that the American Gramophone Company were seeking to gain control of the British Columbia Graphophone Company. Although the nominal capital of the British company was nearly twice that of the American concern, the latter had recently been acquired by the Radio Corporation of America and had itself taken over the Marconiphone Company.

Columbia's Managing Director, Louis Sterling, told reporters that the transfer of shares to buyers in the United States had been taking place at such a rate that now more than 50 per cent of the Company's share capital was held on the other side of the Atlantic. Obviously, if these shares came under the control of one person or one organization, they would have control of the Company. Lord Marks contented himself by saying that the rumours were probably not without foundation, and that a meeting of interested parties was being arranged in Paris. Later, on 5 May, he added that in his opinion a merger between the two companies was both logical and practical. However, three days later at the Radio Corporation of America's AGM, the President, General Harbord, stated that, 'Negotiations for a merger had been broken off entirely.'

The development of the gramophone record industry is one of the great twentieth-century romances of commerce. The Gramophone Company, with its well-known His Master's Voice trade mark, pressed its first record in 1908, at its Hayes, Middlesex, factory. It is said that if all the records produced in its first twenty years' existence were played continuously, they would provide a thousand years' music.

Renewed rumours of a merger between HMV and Columbia became current in March 1930. The former had increased its issued capital to £3.3 million, having a current market value of £13 million. In 1929 its profits amounted to £1,168,217 and the Company paid a 60 per cent dividend on its ordinary shares. The situation at Columbia had remained more static and the profit earnings were disappointing. In March 1930 the issued capital stood at £1.58 million, having market value of £15.4 million. Profits in 1929 amounted to £505,000, and the shareholders were paid a 45 per cent dividend on the ordinary shares.

The struggle ended a year later, in April 1931, a few months before the death of Thomas Edison, the father of the gramophone. It was announced that a new company was being formed to acquire the whole of the share capital of both companies, on the basis of an exchange of shares. The ordinary share capital of the new company, to be known as Electrical & Musical Industries Ltd (EMI), was priced at £6 million, together with £500,000 Preference Shares. Mr Alfred Clark became the Chairman of the new company, and the Directors were Louis Sterling, Managing Director, Lord Marks, J. Broad, E. de Stein, M. Herbert, E. T. L. Williams and D. Sarnoff, the President of the Radio Corporation of America. The articles of association described the objectives of the company as, 'Manufacturers and dealers in apparatus and machinery used in the generation, accumulation and supply of electrical energy, makers of musical, scientific, surgical, therapeutic and medical apparatus and instruments, including machines for recording, reproduction, transmitting or receiving sounds and vision pictures, manufacturers and dealers in gramophones and radio sets, etc.' It is worth noting that these objectives clearly anticipated the introduction and commercialization of television.

One of Lord Marks's last public engagements as a Director of EMI Ltd was a ceremony at Paddington Station in April 1934. The Company hired a special train comprising four specially modified coaches designed to take their radio and gramophone products to their Agents and Dealers throughout the country, without the necessity of inviting them to London. Greatly to Lord Marks's delight he persuaded his old friend Ramsay MacDonald to come along and wave the guard's green flag, sending the train off on its 3000-mile journey.

In June 1937, when Louis Sterling received his knighthood, Lord Marks presided over a splendid celebration dinner held at the Savoy Hotel, when a large portrait in oils of Lady Sterling was presented to him. In his speech Sir Louis said that he and Lord Marks had been indefatigably associated in the interests of the gramophone industry, and that there was no doubt that the charm and strength of character of his old friend had been a tower of strength during the many vicissitudes of the Columbia Company.

Lord Marks continued to play an active rôle in the work of the

The presentation of Lady Sterling's portrait.

London Chamber of Commerce. In 1933 he successfully stood again as a Council Member at the 51st Annual General Meeting. He also accompanied Sir Arthur Balfour, the Chairman of the British National Committee of the International Chamber of Commerce, to the Biennial Conference in Washington. He made an important contribution, speaking on the question of barriers to maritime transportation and trade marks.

In 1935 Lord Marks was invited to become President of the Institute of Fuel, and in his Presidential Address he advocated, 'The creation by Act of Parliament of a permanent central body to co-ordinate the whole of the power and heating requirements of the country.' He suggested the need for a national policy for the conservation of coal resources, cheapening, facilitating and widening the use of coal, and developing coal as a raw material for oil and chemical products. Fifty years on, politicians of both the left and the right have failed to create a National Policy for fuel. Huge investments of public funds have been made in individual sections of the fuel industry, but still we are without any co-ordinated National Plan for energy resources. The largely foreign-dominated oil lobby remains extremely powerful, and the sudden Arab-inspired rise in oil prices in the last decade caused a staggering blow to our economy. The OPEC countries have acquired vast wealth

Holiday scene at Bexhill.

without responsibility, and this money has been allowed to float around the world doing infinite damage to exchange systems and trade. In the United Kingdom we have been compelled to dissipate our new-found wealth in the North Sea in order to finance social security and unemployment benefits. There are many people today who believe that a national fuel policy, as advocated by Lord Marks nearly fifty years ago, would have greatly improved our present-day competitiveness in world markets, and to some extent mitigated the disastrous increases in world oil prices.

Chapter 8
George Croydon Marks – the Man

In middle life Lord Marks was described as being of medium height, having dark hair with deep-set eyes, and a Celtic appearance. By the time he was fifty his hair, bushy eyebrows and beard had turned white, and he acquired a well-rounded, portly figure. He was an elegant man and always dressed formally in well-cut clothes. He was rarely seen without his black homburg hat, and only when relaxing at home did he allow himself the concession of wearing a soft felt trilby hat. He retained his Celtic temperament and non-conformist attitudes throughout his life and was always immensely kind, warm-hearted and loyal to his friends and colleagues. He became an old hand at the art of making delightful and witty speeches, whilst retaining the ability to express himself forcefully and succinctly.

He loved entertaining his friends, and was always a delightful host and extremely congenial to those who made his acquaintance. He never tired of travelling and his many crossings of the Atlantic were highlights in his busy and varied career. He enjoyed good living, but was always a very private person, and in the social sense persistently kept out of the news. He enjoyed the company of the opposite sex and liked nothing better than the opportunity of escorting young ladies on a tour of inspection of his beautiful garden. In later life his garden, collecting antiques and surrounding himself with beautiful things, became his main forms of relaxation. It was his habit to go off alone on Saturday mornings to browse the local antique-shops, causing Lady Marks much apprehension, because she never knew what he would be bringing home next to fill their already very adequately furnished and beautiful home.

Prior to World War I Lord and Lady Marks lived at 'St Bernards', an elegant Victorian house in Caterham, Surrey. During the War they removed nearer to London, to 'Rothbury', Blackheath Park in South East London, and it was whilst living in Blackheath that they acquired 'Panarvor', their holiday home at Bude in North Devon. In 1914 they moved their principal residence to 'Carrick

Carrick Grange, Sevenoaks.

Grange', a large early Victorian mansion, standing in 10 acres just outside Sevenoaks in Kent. It was at this time that Lord Marks became interested in horticulture, and he created a magnificent Japanese garden in the grounds of 'Carrick Grange'. In 1932 his head gardener, L. B. Cannon, was awarded the coveted Chalmers Challenge Cup for Japanese blooms. Concurrently with the move to Sevenoaks, Lord Marks leased for twelve months a holiday home at Eastbourne known as 'Hollywell Mount', and the following year he acquired a house at Bexhill named 'Baskerville', which he retained until they removed to Bournemouth in 1933. Queenie Usher's children still have many happy holiday photographs taken during their annual visits to Bexhill.

Throughout the period 1924 to 1933 Lord Marks lived in his Lincoln's Inn Fields flat from Monday to Friday, returning home to Lady Marks and his much-loved garden at the weekends. One suspects that in middle life his relationship with Lady Marks became one of toleration rather than adoration. Resigning himself to the hard fact that he could not have children of his own distanced him from his wife, although he was always too Christian and courteous in his behaviour to allow this to become apparent to those around him. Their ward, Queenie Usher, was a great solace to both of them and they always derived great pleasure from their many nieces and nephews and their children. Lord Marks was

Lord Marks's favourite Daimler car.

always affectionately called Uncle George by the children and the younger generation called Lady Marks 'Little Grandma'.

Cannon, the head gardener, was one of three key members of their personal staff who remained in their service until Lord Marks's death in 1938. Alec Kernahan, the chauffeur, had three cars in his charge at 'Carrick Grange', a Daimler Landaulet with the famous sleeve-valve engine, an American Essex Super 6, and one of the first Austin 12 saloons. Later, the Essex was exchanged for a splendid new American Buick. When Lord Marks removed to Bournemouth in 1933 the original Daimler was replaced by the latest model with a superbly appointed Hooper body. The third member of the team was Winnie Cole, Lady Marks's personal maid for many years. She came from Romsey in Hampshire, and whenever she paid a visit to her family, she returned laden with lardy cakes, for which her mistress had a great liking.

Sunday in the Marks household is especially well remembered by Queenie Usher's son Michael. It was a strictly religious day, and the only time the cars were used was to take the family to church. After lunch the staff had the remainder of the day free and supper was always a cold collation, prepared in advance, so that the family and their guests could help themselves. Michael Usher recalls with special pleasure that at this meal he and his brother Dennis were allowed to help themselves to not the usual one, but to two, stone jars of their favourite ginger beer.

Throughout his life Lord Marks never wavered in his devotion to the work of the Congregational Church and its affiliated bodies. He was Treasurer of the Sunday School Union for many years and in 1913 held the office of President. The following year he was elected Chairman of the Council of the Union, in succession to his old friend Sir Francis Belsey, whom he first met when as boys they attended Sunday School Conferences at Foots Cray in Kent. At the Union's Annual Conference in 1914 he charmed his audience by relating the story of his encounter with a little girl in Chicago suffering from rheumatic fever. So impressed had he been with the child's faith and courage, that he promised her that no matter where he was, or what he was doing, he would think of her and say a little prayer for her every day at 3 o'clock, adding that he had never failed to keep his promise.

The welfare of children and support for charities concerned with their special needs were always close to his heart. Within days of his elevation to the House of Lords he broadcast an appeal on the radio for a Children's Convalescent Home at Clacton-on-Sea on behalf of the National Sunday School Union. He had been actively involved in the work of the Girls' Life Brigade as its Treasurer, since its formation in 1902. He took the chair at a huge International Rally held in the Albert Hall in 1930, and in a stirring speech described the Brigade's objectives under the headings spiritual, physical, educational and social. Later he took a leading rôle in the reorganization of the Brigade, and was instrumental in the transfer at half its market value of a large house in Buxton to the Salvation Army. In September 1932 Lord and Lady Marks attended the wedding of Ramsay MacDonald's eldest daughter in the little Congregational Church in Wendover. A few weeks later his youngest daughter, Ishbel, was the guest of honour at the Brigade's 30th anniversary celebrations presided over by Lord Marks. This duty became an annual commitment, and his last major public appearance was at the 36th Anniversary Rally, held as usual in the Albert Hall, shortly before his 80th birthday. Upon this occasion he had the honour of welcoming the Duchess of Gloucester as guest of honour. F. A. Creed, Lord Marks's personal assistant at Lincoln's Inn Fields for many years and formerly manager of his publishing company, Technical Records, was for some years the conductor of the Massed Congregational Choir. No doubt, due largely to Creed's intervention, Lord Marks was persuaded to become President of the

Lord Marks greets the Duchess of Gloucester at the Albert Hall.

London Sunday Schools Choir in 1930. However, although the choir diplomatically never forgot to give frequent renderings of his favourite hymn, 'Jerusalem', it was the little church choir at Claygate in Kent for whom he had a special affection.

Lord Marks was a non-smoker and teetotal all his life, but he never insisted upon those around him conforming to his standards. He preferred always to persuade by example. However, he did actively campaign for the retention of the traditional British Sabbath. He maintained that Sunday was a religious day to be spent quietly with the family. In December 1930 he successfully led a delegation organized by the Imperial Alliance for the Defence of Sunday to County Hall, in an endeavour to persuade the London County Council to ban boxing contests and similar events being held on the Sabbath.

In the 1930s, before the advent of the National Health Service, hospitals depended very largely upon voluntary contributions to finance new buildings and modernization. Following his elevation to the House of Lords, Lord Marks actively supported several organizations concerned with the extension of our hospital services. In January 1930 he laid the foundation stone of a new hospital at Holliers Hill in Bexhill and became President of the hospital committee. Later he led the fight for the provision of a new hospital

Cerne Abbas, Bournemouth.

Lord and Lady Marks's Golden Wedding photograph.

at Sevenoaks. Lord Marks maintained always that modern hospitals having the latest facilities should be available to all, irrespective of means, and that this was a question of national responsibility and not charity. Had he lived he would undoubtedly have been an enthusiastic supporter and advocate of the post-war Beveridge Plan.

In July 1931 Lord and Lady Marks celebrated their golden wedding anniversary by giving their many friends a lavish party at the Langham Hotel in London. Lord Marks's old school friends Alexander and Alfred Smith and their wives were specially honoured guests. Alexander had been George Marks's best man, and the two wives had been Lady Marks's bridesmaids. Both the Smith brothers married in 1881, and although they continued to live in Eltham, they never lost touch with their old friends George and Maggie Marks.

In his seventy-fifth year Lord Marks decided to retire to Bournemouth. Recently he had been seen less and less at the office, in the Chamber of the House of Lords, and at his clubs, the Reform and the National Liberal Club. In the summer of 1933 he and Lady Marks removed to 'Oak House', The Avenue, Bournemouth. Shortly after their move, a much larger house named 'Cerne Abbas', on the opposite side of the road, became vacant. Lord

The final Garden Party at Cerne Abbas.

Marks immediately saw the great potential of the then sadly neglected garden, and was often seen crossing the road to stand and ponder the situation. Eventually, in the early part of 1935, without reference to Lady Marks, he purchased the property.

The house, by modern standards, was ridiculously large for occupation by two elderly persons. Built in Edwardian times, it had five large reception rooms, a large conservatory, verandah and balcony, together with a three-storey rectangular tower which gave a splendid panoramic view of the coastline over the surrounding tree-tops. Lord Marks immediately retained five full-time professional gardeners to refurbish the 5-acre grounds. The story is told that upon his return home following a few days' absence, he complained about the slow progress being made. The men protested that they only had five pairs of hands, and Lord Marks retorted, 'Well, get fifty and finish the job quickly, I haven't a lot of time to enjoy it!'

In July 1938 when their magnificent garden was looking at its very best, Lord and Lady Marks gave a garden party which was attended by many old friends and former colleagues. This was Lord Marks's last public appearance, and thereafter his health declined rapidly. He was confined to his bed for a few weeks and died peacefully on Saturday morning, 24 September 1938. The funeral service took place at the Richmond Hill Congregational Church in Bournemouth on the following Wednesday, attended by family and friends and a large gathering of former colleagues and associates representing the many facets of his long and busy life. The service was conducted by the Rev. Dr John Short, followed by interment in the North Bournemouth Cemetery. The committal was taken by the Rev. H. J. Frith.

There can be no better epitaph to his memory than to quote from the sermon given by Dr Short during the funeral service:

'We have gathered together to pay a last tribute of respect and affection to our friend, George Croydon Marks, who was called to his rest and reward on September 24th. It is also a service of triumphant praise and gratitude to God for one who so faithfully served his day and generation.

'His interests and activities took so many forms, it is well-nigh impossible to describe the manifold activities in which our friend was engaged throughout his full and busy life. One so full of vitality was sure to seek many outlets for his energetic spirit, and he was active right up to the beginning of his last illness.

'A very large circle of friends knew him as a Consulting Engineer and Patents expert, and as the senior partner in his own firm, Marks & Clerk. The eminence he achieved in this field, as in many another, was a triumph of character and ability. He was born in a humble home, and brought up by Christian parents who were closely associated with the Congregational denomination. From the first, he was almost entirely dependent on his own efforts to achieve mastery of the subject that most gripped him. He loved to tell how the apprentices at Woolwich Arsenal, at a time when through ill-health he was unable to work, and, indeed, contemplated the possibility that he might not be able to continue his studies, subscribed £4 in order that he might purchase some necessary books. That gesture of friendship made a deep impression upon him, and years later he presented a cheque for £1000 to be invested for a similar purpose for the apprentices of Woolwich Arsenal.

'During his subsequent career he held a large number of responsible posts with various engineering firms and became the author of numerous works dealing with special subjects. He also built up a large business with vast ramifications.

'A second large circle of friends will remember him best for his public services in the political world. The zeal for public service burned within him right to the end of his days. From 1906 to 1924 he sat in the House of Commons as Liberal Member for Launceston, in Cornwall. During the War he performed various services on behalf of the Government, and he held an important post in the Ministry of Munitions. He had already received the honour of a Knighthood in 1911, and for his War services he was awarded the CBE.

'In 1929 he joined the Labour Party, having been attracted by the policy of the late Mr Ramsay MacDonald. In that year he was created a Peer of the Realm with the title, self-chosen, Lord Marks of Woolwich. Those who knew him best can tell you that he accepted the honour in order that he might continue his public service. He refused to allow it to make any essential difference to his mode of life, and remained a humble-minded Christian gentleman.

'One might have thought that such a life was already over-full. But he found time also for personal service in specifically Christian work. He was an ardent Free Churchman, most at home among Congregationalists. His name is well known throughout the entire denomination. For personal reasons he never held any special office in the church organisation, but was a staunch supporter and practical and generous helper of its various causes.

'His special interest lay in the work of the Sunday School, and for many years he held high office in the National Sunday School Union. Again, up to the day of his death, he acted as Treasurer for the Girls' Life Brigade, in which he was deeply interested. Many a story he has told of the influence exerted upon him by his own Sunday School teacher when he was a boy. It is not surprising that in later years he should be deeply interested in all kinds of work among young people. He loved to have young people around him at all times.

'Only a week or two before he fell ill, friends were invited to a Garden Party at his home. He was the life and soul of the party. We shall remember long the speech he made upon that occasion, so well did he seem that we little thought his call would come so soon.

'The tribute would be incomplete without a reference to his long years of married life. He would be the first to insist that the success he enjoyed and the work he was able to do were largely due to the inspiration and companionship of Lady Marks.

'Two stories will shed light on the foundations of his character. When delivering a speech to the girls of Wentworth School, he told how his mother, on the day when he left home to go out in the world, put a Bible into his hands and said, "George, always remember that you are not alone. There is another with you." He remained steadfast in that faith.

'Again, when presiding over the anniversary meeting of our church, he told how he was once responsible for driving a tunnel under a river. He received a message from the engineer on the spot, saying, "We have lost the dead centre." He sent a message stopping all work until he could arrive and make the necessary adjustments.

"This", he said, "is the function of the church, and the meaning of worship. But in the world it is easy to lose the dead-centre and to deviate from the straight line." He urged his listeners to give worship the central place in their lives.

'Such was our friend. He will be sorely missed by a great number of people who were privileged to enjoy his loyalty and affection, his cheery presence and his wise advice. He will always be remembered as a great-hearted Christian gentleman, who in a quiet, unobtrusive way followed in the footsteps of his Master.'

In January 1939 Matthew Atkinson Adam died. He had been the first outsider invited to join the Partnership in 1901. In the same month William Triggs was appointed Senior Partner of Marks & Clerk, thus marking the beginning of a new era in the history of this remarkable firm. One of the first acts of the new Partnership was once again to become Chartered Patent Agents by renewing their membership of the Institution.

Lord Marks left an Estate valued at £136,948, and shortly after the Estate had been settled, Lady Marks moved to a smaller house in West Bournemouth named 'Robinswood', where she lived until her death in January 1945. The story is told that in her declining years of widowhood she became very demanding of those around her, especially her ward, Queenie Usher, who she frequently visited in Sutton Coldfield. She refused to stay in the Usher family home, but preferred to reside in the nearby Moor Hall Country Club, accompanied by her maid. During these visits she habitually telephoned the eccentric Dr John Morgan in the Birmingham office, requesting he let her have some 'spending money', because she loathed making personal visits to a Bank. The dialogue was always the same.

'John, please arrange to let me have some cash.'

'Certainly, Lady Marks,' he replied, 'I think we can manage £10 from the Petty Cash.'

'Don't be silly, John,' she retorted, 'I require at least £100 at once.' Without a further word of protest the cash was always forthcoming.

Index

Page numbers in italic type refer to illustrations.